RESOLVED
Primer

A Look into the 13 Resolutions

ORRIN WOODWARD
with JOHN DAVID MANN

RESOLVED *Primer*

A Look into the 13 Resolutions

ORRIN WOODWARD
WITH JOHN DAVID MANN

First Edition, October 2012

Published by:
Obstaclés Press Inc.
4072 Market Place Dr.
Flint, MI 48507

http://www.orrinwoodward.com

*Cover design and layout by
Norm Williams - http://www.nwa-inc.com*

Printed in the United States of America

Dedication

Many will browse this book, and a good number will even read it cover to cover, but only a small minority will thoroughly absorb these thirteen resolutions and apply them to the fabric of their everyday lives.

It is for those rare few, those who yearn to be champions, those who deeply hunger to find their purpose, reach their potential, and fulfill their destiny, that these pages are aimed.

You know who you are.

This book is for *you*.

Table of Contents

Introduction

Resolve to perform what you ought. Perform
without fail what you resolve.
— Benjamin Franklin

In the early eighteenth century, three young Colonial Americans resolved to build lives of virtue by studying and applying daily resolutions. Each of these three men made his life count, creating a legacy of selfless thoughts, words, and deeds.

- The first, through tireless sacrificial leadership, and against indescribable odds, defeated the mighty British Empire with his ragtag group of colonial volunteers.

- The second, through his growing international fame, sterling character, and endless tact, became America's leading diplomat, forming international alliances that secured war funding, without which, the Colonials' cause would have been doomed.

- The third, through his overwhelming intellectual and spiritual gifts, became Colonial America's greatest minister, who, by preaching and writing, fanned the flames of the spiritual renewal called the Great Awakening, which led to further political and economic freedoms on the heels of the American Revolution.

George Washington, Benjamin Franklin, and Jonathan Edwards are three examples of great individuals who succeeded in transforming themselves by diligently studying and applying a set of personal resolutions. In the process, they each created an enduring legacy not only through what they did, but also, and perhaps more importantly, through who they *were*.

That is, in a nutshell, the purpose of the little book you hold in your hands. These resolutions are designed as a set of core principles for your daily study—meditations, if you will, aimed at helping to sharpen, define, and refine your fundamental character. Here are several dictionary definitions of the word *resolve*:

1. To come to a definite or earnest decision about; determine (to do something): *I have resolved that I shall live to the full.*
2. To deal with (a question, a matter of uncertainty, etc.) conclusively; settle; solve: *to resolve the question before the board.*
3. *Music:* to cause (a voice part or the harmony as a whole) to progress from a dissonance to a consonance.

When you apply the thirteen resolutions consistently in your daily life, you will see all three of these definitions fulfilled.

Written resolutions should encompass the whole person; they are a plan for developing your character and thinking from who you are to who you desire to be. When you write and study these resolutions, you resolve to live internally what you proclaim externally.

There is, however, a challenge.

If success were as simple as writing a few resolutions and studying them daily, well then, success would be a simple matter! Yet the individuals who are able to genuinely incorporate such principles—the Washingtons, Franklins, and Edwardses—are a precious few. Everyone in America has New Year's resolutions on January 1, but few lead to lasting personal transformation (or even significant weight control!) as most are abandoned even before the following month begins.

Dr. Martyn Lloyd-Jones explains why only a few achieve lasting success in their resolutions:

> Man is a wonderful creature, he is mind, he is heart, and he is will. Those are the three main constituents of man. God has given him a mind, He has given him a heart, He has given him a will whereby he can act.

Ah, and there is the challenge. True personal change is not a matter of mental exercise, or of emotional experience, or of disciplined attention. It is a matter of *all three at once*. Transforming your life requires that your whole person— mind, heart, and will—be engaged in the process.

Some may read the resolutions and make a mental nod of approval, but not involve the heart or will. Others may become inspired by what they read—on fire, their hearts are touched. But without engagement of the mind and will, what will that accomplish?

Resolutions must absorb the mind, touch the heart, and engage the will to produce deep, lasting change.

The good news is that anyone *can* do this. *Anyone* who desires to do so can engage and marry all three faculties together in the pursuit of these resolutions.

It is not a quick process and will likely not occur in a single reading. Repetition is an essential ingredient, both because it is so often on one's second and third readings that the greatest insights reveal themselves, and also because while one reading is enough to engage the *conscious* mind, it is the sacrament of repetition that engages the subconscious (as we will explore in the course of resolution 4).

That is why this book is designed for you to use as a one-year program.

Studying one resolution a week, applying all of that chapter's principles and directives in your daily life throughout the seven days of that week, will take you thirteen weeks, which is exactly one-quarter of a year. Repeating the cycle will allow you to thoroughly explore all thirteen resolutions four times over the space of one calendar year.

In one year, your life will transform.

The resolutions are also grouped into three sections: private achievements, public achievements, and leadership achievements. This order represents a natural progression, since private victories by necessity precede public ones, and the combination of these two levels of victory creates a level of character and competence that produces leadership.

The thirteen resolutions take you through the entire process, from private to public to leadership success. The goal is to engender wisdom by learning how to apply the right principles at the right time. Indeed, the ultimate goal for any person learning and applying the thirteen resolutions is to develop wisdom for *life*.

Private Achievements

1. PURPOSE: I resolve to discover my God-given purpose.
   I know that when my potential, passions, and profitability intersect, my purpose is revealed.

2. CHARACTER: I resolve to choose character over reputation any time they conflict.
   I know that my character is who I am, while my reputation is only what others say that I am.

3. ATTITUDE: I resolve to have a positive attitude in all situations.
   I know that by listening to my positive voice and turning down my negative voice, I will own a positive attitude.

4. ALIGNMENT: I resolve to align my subconscious mind with my conscious intention.
   I know that ending the civil war between these two is crucial for everything I seek to achieve.

Public Achievements

5. PRACTICE: I resolve to develop and implement a game plan in each area of my life.
   I know that planning and doing are essential parts of the success process.

6. SCORE: I resolve to keep score in the game of life.
   I know that the scoreboard forces me to check and confront my results and make needed adjustments in order to win.

7. FRIENDSHIP: I resolve to practice the art and science of friendship.
   I know that everyone needs a true friend to lighten the load when life gets heavy.

8. FINANCIAL INTELLIGENCE: I resolve to practice financial intelligence.
   I know that over time, my wealth compounds when my net income is higher than my expenses.

Leadership Achievements

9. LEADERSHIP: I resolve to practice the art and science of leadership.
   I know that everything rises and falls based on the leadership culture created in my community.

10. UNITY: I resolve to practice the art and science of conflict resolution.
    I know that unresolved conflicts can destroy a community's unity and growth.

11. HOLISM: I resolve to practice big-picture thinking.
    I know that by viewing life as interconnected patterns rather than isolated events, I can accomplish big things.

12. RESILIENCE: I resolve to increase my capacity to overcome adversity.
    I know that fulfilling my vision depends on my perseverance in the face of obstacles and setbacks.

13. LEGACY: I resolve to leave a legacy by fulfilling my purpose.
    I know that by reversing the natural currents of decline in the world, I will have a positive impact on the world that continues beyond the limits of my life.

Imagine each of these resolutions as an instrument in an orchestra. Each plays beautiful music, but when they work together they produce a masterpiece, a living symphony of success. This book offers the instruments to play life's symphonic masterpiece.

There is an inscription on a bishop's tomb in Westminster Abbey:

When I was young and free and my imagination had no limits, I dreamed of changing the world.

As I grew older and wiser, I discovered the world would not change, so I shortened my sights somewhat and decided to change only my country, but it too seemed immovable.

As I grew into my twilight years, in one last desperate attempt, I settled for changing only my family, those closest to me, but alas, they would have none of it.

And now I realize as I lie on my deathbed, if I had only changed myself first, then by example I would have changed my family. From their inspiration and encouragement, I would then have been able to better my country and, who knows, I may have even changed the world.

We cannot hope to influence others until we have come to profoundly influence ourselves. By beginning with yourself and forging these resolutions into your being, you become a living model of your principles and a change agent for those around you.

Resolve to master the principles in these pages and to be transformed by the wisdom gained from your journey. By transforming yourself, you will gain the tools, the competence, and, more importantly, the character to transform your community, and with those things, the means to change the world—bold words, I know, but true.

Opportunity is knocking. Seize it. Open the door and claim your destiny.

PURPOSE
"I resolve to discover my God-given purpose."

*They say there are two important days in your life:
the day you were born, and the day you
find out* why *you were born.*
— Carl Townsend

Imagine you are part of a basketball game with two teams, a regulation court of smooth, shiny maple planks, and a brand-new eight-panel ball—but no hoop. Up and down the court you go, dribbling the ball, passing it back and forth expertly...but somehow, you never seem to really get anywhere.

Doesn't this describe the way so many people go through the motions of their lives—running around furiously busy yet never accomplishing anything of consequence?

A life without purpose is just like a basketball game without a hoop.

Once you place hoops on life's backboards though, everything changes. The point of the game suddenly becomes clear. All at once, there is meaning to all that running up and down the court: It's to score points by putting the ball in the hoop! What moments ago seemed like a gigantic waste of energy now becomes an activity with the specific intent of accomplishing purposeful objectives.

This is what purpose does in a person's life. Purpose provides direction, filling every task, even seemingly mundane ones, with significance. Dr. Myles Monroe, chairman of the Third World Leaders Association and author of *Kingdom Principles*, describes it beautifully:

> The poor man, the rich man, the black man, the white man—every person has a dream in his heart. Your vision may already be clear to you, or it may still be buried somewhere deep in your heart, waiting to be discovered. Fulfilling this dream is what gives purpose and meaning to life.

A Litmus Test for Purpose

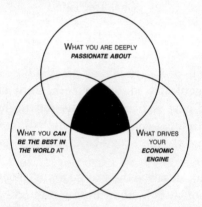

Why were you created? What is the purpose of your life?

In *Good to Great*, Jim Collins describes his extensive research into the key factors that make certain companies consistently outperform the competition and become truly great. At the heart of his findings lies what Collins calls the Hedgehog Concept. The term comes from the tortoise-and-hare-like fable of the fox and the hedgehog. No matter how quickly or craftily the wily fox attempts to get at the hedgehog, the little animal has a strategy that works every time: it rolls itself into an untouchable, spiky little ball.

As Collins reports, an exceptional company performs absolutely consistently—like the hedgehog. He describes the impenetrable ball it rolls itself into as consisting of three overlapping circles, which focus on a product or service that:

1. *outshines all its competitors*
2. *drives its economic engine*
3. *it is passionate about*

Great companies are those that learn to apply that three-part litmus test to everything they do and then exercise the relentless discipline to say "No, thank you" to everything that fails the test.

As individuals, we can do that, too. Collins writes:

> Suppose you were able to construct a work life that meets the following three tests: First, you are doing work for which you have a genetic or God-given talent. ("I feel that I was just born to be doing this.") Second, you are well paid for what you do. ("I get paid to do this? Am I dreaming?") Third, you are doing work you are passionate about and absolutely love to do, enjoying the actual process for its own sake. ("I look forward to getting up and throwing myself into my daily work, and I really believe in what I'm doing.")

The good news is *you can*. That's exactly what it means to *discover your purpose*.

Consider every pursuit you are engaged in or have thought about becoming engaged in. Which ones engage your *passion* (or motivation), your *potential* (your God-given gifts and abilities), and your *profitability* (the unfettered function of your economic engine)?

It is when you find the pursuit that makes all three circles intersect that you are living a purposeful life and on the path to fulfilling your destiny.

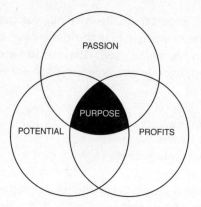

1) Passion

All great achievements are attained through passion. Without passion, you will never stick it out when the going gets tough: The criticisms, setbacks, and external pressures will wear you down before long. It is passion that keeps us going in the face of seemingly insurmountable odds and enables us to refuse to quit no matter what. Passion is non-negotiable.

What would you spend your days doing if you could do anything at all? What would you do if you were so wealthy you'd never have to work another day for pay? What is that thing you would do every day for the rest of your life, even if it never paid you a dime?

Sometimes it is something about the world that angers or frustrates us, a wrong we want to right or a lack we want to fill, that leads to the passion of purpose. That was the case with William Wilberforce, who spent his life overturning the institution of slavery in England (an example soon followed by Lincoln and the United States), and with Gandhi, who dedicated his to liberating all of India.

Sometimes it is simply the love of something that drives us to pursue it to the point of excellence.

Wally Amos loved chocolate chip cookies. As a talent agent, he would send his home-baked cookies to potential clients to entice them to meet with him and consider signing with his agency. (It worked, too; this was how he came to represent Simon and Garfunkel.) Wally enjoyed being an agent, but his passion was cookies. Finally, on the advice and encouragement of friends, he opened a cookie store in Los Angeles. In his first year of operation, he sold $300,000 worth of cookies, and the next year, his sales topped $1 million. Wally eventually became a multimillionaire, and Famous Amos became one of the most recognized cookie brand names in the world.

He achieved meteoric success—all for the love of a good cookie.

2) Potential

In this famous passage from *A Return to Love*, Marianne Williamson beautifully evokes the nearly limitless potential every human being holds:

> Our deepest fear is not that we are inadequate. Our deepest fear is that we are powerful beyond measure. It is our light, not our darkness that most frightens us. We ask ourselves, "Who am I to be brilliant, gorgeous, talented, and fabulous?" Actually, who are you not to be? You are a child of God. Your playing small does not serve the world. There is nothing enlightened about shrinking so that other people won't feel insecure around you. We are all meant to shine, as children do. We were born to make manifest the glory of God that is within us. It's not just in some of us; it's in everyone.

The greatest treasures on earth can be found in the numerous cemeteries across the world: There lie the buried potentials of the multitude who played it safe their whole lives. But there is nothing safe about "playing it safe." Doing so only ensures that you will never reach your potential or fulfill your purpose. None of us is making it out of here alive anyway. Doesn't it make sense to reach for greatness?

What are *your* unique gifts? What skills and abilities do you bring to the table that can benefit the world?

Wally Amos didn't just love cookies; he also knew how to make them. A beloved aunt taught him her secret recipe, and he improved upon it. As an agent, he was good. But as a cookie master, he was *great*.

3) Profitability

Profitability, the third Hedgehog Circle, simply means the ability to turn your potential and passion into a fruitful calling.

You might think that such a mundane notion as *profit* doesn't belong in a discussion of something as lofty as life's purpose. But without creating a viable economic engine, you won't be able to pursue that passion or potential for long. Why not? Because pesky little details will keep getting in the way—details like food, beverages, and housing accommodations.

In a free society, people will reward you financially only when they are satisfied with the products or services you offer, and your economic engine will run at full throttle only when *enough* people do so. If Wally Amos's passion had been for something that few wanted—say, he'd been a purveyor of fine chicken livers, or a connoisseur of parsnip stew—we probably would never have heard of him. But who doesn't love cookies?

By pursuing your passion and potential *and* filling a viable customer need, you can thrive even in today's "flat" world. The corporate cradle-to-grave kinds of jobs we remember from the twentieth century may be gone, but serving customers' needs will never go out of style. In fact, serving customers' needs is more important today than ever because in today's market, customers are better informed and competition comes from all over the globe.

Big Rocks First

Living a life of purpose means learning how to focus your *time* on purpose. Time is the stuff life is made of.

Hyrum Smith, the creator of the legendary Franklin Planner, writes in *The 10 Natural Laws of Successful Time and Life Management*:

> Time is just like money. When you decide to spend one hour watching TV, you have also decided not to spend the time on what? Everything else. You would be very upset if someone gained access to your bank account and stole all your money. Most people, though, don't blink an eye when all sorts of culprits sneak into their lives and steal their time.

Smith once asked a group of executives why, if they felt reading was important, they weren't reading more. After an uncomfortably long silence, one fellow in the back row spoke up: "Books don't ring." What a great insight! Books don't grab you and say, "Hey, *read* me." Reading is a purposeful and profoundly *important* activity, but not an *urgent* one.

Stephen R. Covey describes the difference between urgent and important this way:

> Urgent matters are usually visible. They press on us; they insist on action. They're often popular with others. They're usually right in front of us. And often they are pleasant, easy, and fun to do. But so often unimportant! Importance, on the other hand, has to do with results. If something is important, it contributes to your mission, your values, your high priority goals.

Genuinely urgent matters need to be attended to right away, but many high-priority items in our lives are not urgent—in other words, they don't *have* to be done this instant. Unless we exercise the discipline to set aside the time it will take to attend to them, they will never get done.

In *First Things First*, Covey illustrates the importance of priorities by describing a simple demonstration.

The presenter sets out a wide-mouth jar and fills it to the top with fist-sized rocks. Then he asks his audience, "Is the jar full?" It's obvious that no more rocks can fit, so they reply that yes, it's full. But is it? The presenter then pulls out a bucket of coarse gravel and starts adding it, shaking the jar so it fills in the spaces between the rocks. Again he asks, "Is the jar full?" A little more wary, the audience hesitates. It *looks* full...but it looked full before, too. Now the presenter pulls out a bucket of sand, and the audience laughs. Apparently the jar is not full yet because he easily pours in a good amount of sand. And even then, it isn't full, as he shows by grabbing a pitcher of water and pouring that in, too.

What is the point of the demonstration? "If you work at it," suggests one participant, "you can always fit more into your life?"

"No," says the presenter. "The point is this: If he'd started out by filling the jar with gravel and sand first, how many rocks would he have been able to add? *Not one.*"

Those rocks are the important things in our lives, those that move us closer to the fulfillment of our purpose. The gravel, sand, and water are everything else—the endless tasks, errands, distractions, little crises, and seemingly urgent issues that so easily fill the jars of our days, if we let them. If we don't take care to put the big rocks in first, attending to the truly important things before all the distractions fill up our day, then we'll never get to them.

Choose Your Priorities

This is one of the simplest and most powerful secrets to a successful life: If you cannot manage your time, then you cannot lead your life. Instead, life will lead you.

Effective time management is really *priority management*. And it doesn't have to be complicated. It boils down to this: Discover your purpose, and then spend each day working on your most purposeful tasks—the biggest rocks—first. Everything else—*everything*—is gravel, sand, and water.

This means you have to learn to say no to the merely *good*, so that you will have time to say yes to the *great*. Being *busy* is not the goal; being *purposeful* is. Focus on those assignments you are uniquely qualified to perform, and learn to delegate to others as much of the rest as you can.

When you say, "I don't have time for that," it isn't really true; it's that you haven't prioritized your time for that activity. Warren Buffett has no more hours in his day than the same twenty-four the poorest person has in his. What they each *do* with those twenty-four hours is what makes the difference. Laser-like focus, the ability to narrow options to the essential few, is crucial for all successful people.

As Malcolm Gladwell explains in his bestselling book *Outliers*, mastering any activity requires about ten thousand hours of practice. What great news! This means that potentially you can become a master in practically any field you like, simply by applying yourself. But it also means you cannot be a master in *all* fields. There simply aren't enough ten-thousand-hour slots available in the days and years of your life.

The question you need to ask yourself is this:

What is so worth it to me—what so completely and accurately fulfills my passion, my potential, and my profitability—that I'm willing to pour ten thousand hours of my life into it?

CHARACTER
"I resolve to choose character over reputation any time they conflict."

Character is like a tree and reputation its shadow. The shadow is what we think of it; the tree is the real thing.
— Abraham Lincoln

Character is a special quality that enhances all other virtues. In truth, without character, none of the other resolutions really matter because living without character is like building a house on quicksand.

In the course of your life, you will face situations where you have to make a choice between character and reputation. In order to make the right choice, it's important to understand the two essential virtues that make up the quality of unassailable character.

Integrity

The first of these key ingredients is integrity. The word integrity comes from the Latin *integer*, meaning "whole, complete, and untouched." Being a person of integrity means you are whole, not fragmented or self-contradictory; your words and actions are not in conflict. As Dr. Seuss's noble elephant put it so memorably in *Horton Hatches the Egg*:

I meant what I said
And said what I meant...
An elephant's faithful
One hundred percent!

Yet character is more than what a person *says* or *does*. Character is who the person *is*.

Integrity ensures that a person does not intentionally do wrong. People of integrity may still be criticized, but they can rightfully expect to be believed and trusted—and when they're not, they let time prove them right.

Words such as *honorable, honest, trustworthy, dutiful,* and *faithful* describe a person with integrity. Author Mark Sanborn describes integrity as an essential ingredient of leadership:

> When integrity ceases to be a leader's top priority, when a compromise of ethics is rationalized away as necessary for the "greater good," when achieving results becomes more important than the means to their achievement—that is the moment when a leader steps onto the slippery slope of failure.

John Wooden's Three Principles

In the early years of the twentieth century, an Indiana farmer named Joshua Wooden taught his young family the meaning of integrity, and his son John carried these lessons with him throughout his life. As an adult, John became one of the most revered coaches of all time, winning ten NCAA titles in his last twelve years, including a record seven in a row.

Even more than his winning record, John Wooden was admired for the way he taught and inspired his players to live lives of integrity. Coach Wooden based his life and conduct on three inviolable principles he learned from his father:

1. Never lie.
2. Never cheat.
3. Never steal.

Imagine how simple life would be if everyone followed these principles! Taken together, they form a yardstick against which any person of conscience and character may measure his own actions.

1) Never Lie

People often fall into the habit of bending or misrepresenting the truth because they hope to paint themselves in a better light—to "improve upon the truth." But truth is not improvable; truth is simply truth.

When you are more concerned with your reputation than with your integrity, it becomes tempting to choose what can at times seem to be the easier path: exaggerating, modifying, or twisting the truth—in a word, *lying*—in order to end up looking better in the eyes of others, rather than facing the truth and presenting things simply as they are.

Jack Canfield offers a wonderful insight into the mindset behind this insidious habit:

> In reality, lying is the product of low self-esteem—
> the belief that you and your abilities are not good
> enough to get what you want...the false belief
> that you cannot handle the consequences of people
> knowing the truth about you—which is simply
> another way of saying, *I am not good enough*.

Once you crack open the door to lying, it becomes progressively easier to push that door farther open. Lies warp the liar's character over time, as truth and fiction become confused in his own mind. As Walter Scott wrote many years ago in his epic poem *Marmion*:

Oh! What a tangled web we weave
When first we practice to deceive!

Tell the truth, the whole truth, and nothing but the truth, not only when you speak to others but also when you speak to *yourself*. If you are constantly lying to yourself—for example, making excuses, declaring promises you know you'll never keep, or casting blame rather than acknowledging responsibility—then you will never speak the truth consistently to others.

Don't let yourself be deceived; internal lies always lead to external ones. As C. S. Lewis observed:

When a man is getting better he understands more clearly the evil that is still left in him....A moderately bad man knows he is not very good; a thoroughly bad man thinks he is all right.

2) Never Cheat

As lying is sometimes excused as "just bending the truth," cheating often begins with the temptation to "bend the rules a little." But moral principles do not bend as readily as people seem to hope they will. Instead, they break.

Cheating can appear to be a shortcut to success, but it is always a dead end. Ironically, people who cheat end up hurting themselves in the long run since no one will trust a person who is a cheater. The person who cheats others cheats himself out of his own integrity. In Plato's *Gorgias*, Socrates says:

If it were necessary to do or to suffer injustice, I would choose rather to suffer than to do injustice.

Tennis pro Andy Roddick displayed tremendous integrity in a 2005 Italia Masters tournament in Rome. The game had arrived at match point, meaning one more point and Roddick would win. His opponent Fernando Verdasco hit his second serve, and it was called *out* by the line judge.

In a move as rare as it was noble, Roddick refused to accept the point. Instead, he explained to the line judge that the serve was actually *in*, pointing to a faint indentation on the clay court directly on the white line. Verdasco, having conceded defeat, had already moved to the net, believing the match was over, but Roddick would not "cheat" his way to victory. His integrity was worth more to him than a win he hadn't earned.

Impressed by Roddick's honesty, the line judge overruled his own call. The game resumed, and Verdasco soon came from behind and eventually won the match. But Roddick won an even bigger victory: he claimed his integrity.

Roddick's remarkable sportsmanship is now part of ethics history. Stephen M. R. Covey calls it "Roddick's choice," the ability to demonstrate integrity even when it is costly to do so.

3) Never Steal

One of the biggest factors in declining productivity today is an epidemic of stealing. Robert Half Legal, a premier personnel agency for the legal profession, has calculated that time theft alone costs the American economy approximately $70 billion a year—equivalent to the annual revenues of many of the world's largest companies.

One aspect of this economic scourge is *time theft*, the deliberate actions of employees to misuse or waste time while on the company clock, which causes permanent damage in productivity. Many who would probably never consider stealing directly from their employers' wallets or purses have no qualms about stealing from them indirectly by wasting time and wages.

Why? What's the difference? Perhaps it's simply because the latter is easy to get away with, while the former is far riskier. But if one's only reason for not stealing is the fear of getting caught, then one's integrity is in serious need of repair.

As with cheating, the person who steals may gain materially in the short run, but he robs his own character, which ultimately leads to the worst of consequences in the long run.

Courage

Character starts with integrity, but to fulfill its high calling, it also requires a second ingredient. To have strong character, integrity is *necessary* but not *sufficient*. One can have unimpeachable integrity yet still not have character.

On the school playground, Jack bullies Billy, a younger boy who cannot defend himself. Tom watches this unfold but does not participate. By refusing to join in the bullying, Tom has displayed integrity—but not character.

What would it have taken for Tom to display character? Mustering the courage to step up and defend the younger boy would have displayed character.

Courage is the second critical ingredient of character. Here is the formula:

Character = Integrity × Courage

Even a person of integrity, if she lacks the courage of her convictions, will fail the test when her highest principles are challenged. It is only when our integrity and core principles are challenged by a threat to our comfort and safety that our true level of character reveals itself.

Ella Wheeler Wilcox, famous for her immortal couplet "Laugh and the whole world laughs with you / Weep, and you weep alone," also wrote:

> To sin by silence when they should protest makes cowards of men.

When you hold fast to your principles, even in the face of conflict with others who would violate those principles, you move from integrity to character. Integrity is *not doing wrong*; character is *doing what is right*. Refusing to do wrong (integrity) is good. Having the courage to do right (character) is even better.

Most people would rather opt for relative peace and security than take a stand against injustice, especially if the injustice is not directed toward them. Perhaps they do not fully grasp that by failing to respond, they actually support and help further that injustice. Reverend Martin Niemöller, a Nazi prison camp survivor, beautifully captured this slippery slope of moral compromise:

> First they came for the Communists,
>   and I did not speak out because I was not a Communist.
> Then they came for the Social Democrats,
>   and I did not speak out because I was not a Social Democrat.
> Then they came for the trade unionists,
>   and I did not speak out because I was not a trade unionist.
> Then they came for the Jews,
>   and I did not speak out because I was not a Jew.
> At last they came for me—
>   and there was no one left to speak out for me.

The Perils of Pragmatism

Even in leaders at the highest levels of society's institutions, we often see people's courage blunted by the force of *pragmatism*, the sacrifice of one's higher principles for short-term gains. In his book *Trust: The One Thing that Makes or Breaks a Leader*, executive search expert Les Csorba describes the debilitating effects of pragmatism:

When we follow leaders without a moral compass interested in only results, get ready for the ditch. The ditch into which modern leadership has fallen is the pit of pragmatism.

Many confuse pragmatism with compromise, but they are not the same thing.

The ability to bend on one's position and arrive at a compromise can, in certain circumstances, be itself an act of strong character. At other times, it can be character suicide. What's the difference? It depends on what particulars, principles, or values one lets go of in order to achieve the compromise.

Yale Law School professor Stephen L. Carter succinctly describes the difference this way:

> Compromises that advance high principles are acceptable; those that do not advance high principles are not.

A person of integrity amplified by courage accepts only noble compromises—those that sacrifice one's own comfort, security, or personal gains in order to advance the greater good.

How do we know which is which? That is, how do we know which principles we cannot allow ourselves to sacrifice, no matter what?

For example, who *says* stealing is wrong? What if 51 percent of the people voted in favor of stealing: Would that make it right? Of course, it wouldn't. Moral absolutes are not based on votes; they are based on the moral order inherent in the world.

The Judeo-Christian tradition based on the Ten Commandments provides a time-honored lens through which we are able to see the eternal moral underpinnings of the universe. (Wooden's three principles are direct translations of three of the ten.) Other examples of such glimpses of the absolute are the Golden Rule ("Do unto others as you would have them do unto you") and the medical profession's Hippocratic Oath (popularly simplified as "First, do no harm").

Each of us must develop our own moral grid to live by, just as John Wooden did. Without that matrix of moral absolutes, a compass to discern right from wrong, anything becomes permissible, and our character can easily be eroded by the corrupting influence of pragmatism, relativism, and moral compromise.

The Forge of Character

One cannot develop character simply by reading about it, thinking about it, or talking about it (although all of these can certainly help). Character can only be forged in the pursuit of one's purpose and through the inevitable challenges this brings.

If David had not had to muster the courage to face Goliath, his true character would never have been revealed, and he would have remained an unknown shepherd boy instead of becoming the king of Israel. If we never test ourselves by seizing the opportunity to confront, learn from, and rise above our own Goliaths, we will never become the kings and queens of our own lives.

In J. R. R. Tolkien's *The Lord of the Rings: The Two Towers*, there is a wonderful example of genuine courage emerging in the face of conflict:

> FRODO. I can't do this, Sam.
> SAM.   I know. It's all wrong. By rights we shouldn't
> even be here. But we are. It's like in the
> great stories, Mr. Frodo. The ones that
> really mattered. Full of darkness and
> danger they were....Folk in those stories
> had lots of chances of turning back, only
> they didn't. They kept going. Because they
> were holding on to something.

FRODO. What are we holding onto, Sam?

SAM.   That there's some good in this world, Mr.
       Frodo...and it's worth fighting for.

ATTITUDE
"I resolve to have a positive attitude in all situations."

*I am convinced that life is 10 percent what
happens to me and 90 percent how I react to it.*
— Chuck Swindoll

Jeb, an avid duck hunter, bought a new bird dog for a tidy sum, an amount that his perennially ill-tempered friend Dewhurst told him was way too much.

"Ya got soaked," muttered his friend, and that was the end of the conversation.

Shortly thereafter, Jeb made a startling discovery: His new dog could actually walk on water! Certain that Dewhurst would never believe this news, he decided that rather than tell him, he would invite his buddy out hunting so he could see for himself.

As they waited on the shore behind their duck blinds, a flock of ducks flew by. Both men fired, and sure enough, a duck fell to the lake. Jeb's new dog leapt up and jumped out onto the water—but rather than sinking into the water, it trotted across the surface straight out to where the bird had gone under and retrieved its quarry. Then it turned and trotted back toward the hunters with the duck in its jaws and dropped it at Jeb's feet.

Dewhurst took all this in with his customary poker face and didn't say a word. On the drive home, Jeb couldn't help himself. He turned to his friend and said, "So are you telling me you didn't notice anything at all unusual about my new dog?"

"Well," said Dewhurst reluctantly, "I wasn't gonna mention it, but yeah—ya got soaked, alright. The dog can't swim!"

Poor Dewhurst. He is the type of fellow who would snatch defeat from the jaws of victory.

Two Internal Voices

Winners and losers generally have the same information, but they choose to interpret and respond to it differently. They may even experience the exact same event, but what that event *means* depends on what they each tell themselves about it.

For example, painful experiences are common to both achievers and nonachievers, but whether such an experience empowers or disempowers depends on *the story we create* from the experience. Failure is not the result of external events, but of what we tell ourselves about those events—in a word: *attitude*.

You, like all people, have two internal voices. One regards the world through a positive perspective and speaks to you about all the good in every situation. The other sees the world from a negative perspective and whispers to you about all the bad in every situation—what could go wrong, where the problems lie, why this won't work, and what you should be worrying about.

These voices are something like the traditional symbol of theater: a pair of masks representing comedy and tragedy, one laughing and the other crying—two opposite perspectives on life. Which one is true? Whichever one you decide to listen to.

No matter what information or experience you provide, your negative voice will always find a creative way to criticize it. Even if you witness something miraculous—

like a bird dog walking across the surface of a lake—your negative voice will turn it into bad news.

Wooden's Second Set of Three

You cannot entirely eliminate either voice—but you can learn to turn each one up or down. Winners consistently turn up the positive voice and turn down the negative voice, leading to a healthy positive attitude on life.

Joshua Wooden, the aforementioned Indiana farmer, taught his son John a second set of three principles (Coach Wooden called them his father's "two sets of three") designed to tune *out* the negative voice and turn *up* the positive:

1. Never whine.
2. Never complain.
3. Never make excuses.

Keeping these three principles in mind will help you to notice when you are tuning in to your negative voice.

1) Never Whine

Whining is a sure sign that you are consulting your negative voice. When you hear yourself whine, realize that the sound you're hearing first formed as whispered words in your mind and then entered your heart before spilling out over your tongue. It is the signature call of an early infestation of negative thinking.

Whining asks the question, "Why is this happening to me?" When framing the question this way, it is the negative voice one is looking to for an answer. Instead, learn to ask, "What can I learn from this?" a question that typically evokes the positive voice for its answer.

Winners don't search for sympathy through the negative voice; they search for solutions with the positive voice. Winners don't whine. And whiners don't win.

True, there are times when solutions to a present dilemma are not readily apparent or available. Even in such situations, though, there is no reason to turn to the negative voice and whine like a child. Strap the helmet on a little tighter and apply yourself a little more diligently.

2) Never Complain

If whining is the common-cold variety of negative attitudes, then complaining is pneumonia—a deeper and more dangerous infection.

Complaining represents a subtle but insidious shift in thinking. It points the finger at others (and away from oneself) by saying, "Why did *they* do it this way? Why did *they* make things so tough for me?"

Complaining about others becomes a path to evade taking responsibility for solving our own problems. This shift in thinking eventually turns into false beliefs about ourselves: "Why did that happen to me?" becomes "That kind of thing *always* happens to me, so there's no point in even trying."

Worse yet, once we adopt a negative belief, the temptation is great to defend and assert it in the effort to protect our frail egos—which of course only makes that negative belief stronger. In *Illusions*, Richard Bach writes:

Argue for your limitations, and sure enough, they are yours.

Thus, by listening to your negative voice, failure becomes a self-fulfilling prophecy, leading to a life of victimhood and a constant grieving over the unfairness of life.

People of purpose and character resist the temptation to complain and instead address challenging issues head-on, seeking to resolve the matter. They know that once they start complaining, they surrender their capacity to effect positive change.

Complaining leads to bitterness and resentment, while a habit of taking responsibility leads to a life of appreciation and joy.

3) Never Make Excuses

If whining is the common cold of negativity and complaining the pneumonia, then making excuses is tuberculosis—a disease in times past referred to as *consumption*.

People who habitually make excuses have stopped asking questions and replaced them with self-deceiving statements like, "It's not my fault. I couldn't help it. There was nothing I could do about it."

Winners can always find reasons to win. Losers can always find excuses to lose.

Why is it so easy to make excuses for the lack of results? Because excuses provide us with the justification to not change and grow. Blaming and finger-pointing is a coping mechanism—and not a healthy one. It may provide temporary relief from the pain of defeat, but it sets us up in the long term for the far deeper pain of living an unfulfilled life.

People with a positive attitude know that temporary defeats are only stepping stones on the path to success. Thomas Edison was once asked how it felt to fail after his seven-hundredth attempt to perfect the incandescent light bulb. He replied:

> I have not failed seven hundred times. I have succeeded in proving that those seven hundred ways will not work.

I love what Winston Churchill said about the path to success:

> Success is going from one failure to another with no loss in enthusiasm.

Reframing

Another term for turning down the negative voice and turning up the positive voice is *reframing*. The positive voice reframes potential negative events into empowering positive viewpoints, while the negative voice frames everything into disempowering viewpoints—such as with the duck-hunting friend and the miraculous dog.

In *Creators Syndicate*, author Mary Hunt shares a powerful example of reframing. At one point, she was suddenly without a vehicle and had to share her husband's car for six months:

> I felt as if I'd lost my freedom. My wings were clipped; no more spontaneity for me. If I wasn't being "chaperoned" as a passenger in my husband's car, I was having to ask permission to borrow it.

After about three months, it occurred to Hunt that it wasn't the situation that was making her miserable; it was how she was interpreting the situation:

> I wasn't recognizing that the nicest guy in the world was willing to take me anywhere I wanted to go, anytime I wanted to get there.
>
> I decided I had to reframe my thinking. Rather than a pathetic dependent child, I would see myself as a woman of privilege. *I have a driver! Every day, I am driven back and forth to work. I am free to chat, read, write, think, knit, or nap.*
>
> See? A different way of looking at the same situation.

It takes diligent practice to turn down the negative voice and reframe events, especially at first, but it's well worth the effort. It is no exaggeration to say that learning to harness the power of reframing can fundamentally change your life. It can even win a presidential election.

During the 1984 presidential campaign, many were concerned about Ronald Reagan's age, fearful that a man in his mid-seventies would not be able to handle the pressures of the Oval Office. Sure enough, during one debate, a panelist raised the matter of Reagan's age. But Reagan reframed the issue:

> I want you to know, I will not make age an issue in this campaign. I am not going to exploit, for political purposes, my opponent's youth and inexperience.

The audience went wild—in fact, even Walter Mondale, Reagan's opponent, had to laugh. The issue of age did not come up again for the duration of the campaign.

Pulling Mind Weeds

However, there will inevitably be moments when you inadvertently listen to your negative voice. How do you root out the negative thinking planted by that negative voice?

When you listen to your (or someone else's) negative voice, negative thinking starts germinating like weeds in the garden of your mind, blocking out the sun of reason and preventing clear, positive ideas from taking root. If allowed to grow, these weeds will develop root systems throughout your patterns of thought, making eradication ever more difficult. In time, they will choke off your thinking to the point where your life ceases to bear any fruit at all.

Whining, complaining, and excuse-making are the evidence of a robust growth of weeds in the garden of your mind, and negative thinking is the soil that encourages their growth. If you find weeds there, you have only one course of action: Pull them. And do it *now* before they have any more time to put down their insidious roots.

Your mind is *your* garden. *You* are the gardener.

No one can plant weeds in the garden of your mind without your permission. Unfortunately, many grant exactly that permission to everyone around them, from their co-workers and acquaintances to the television they watch, advertisements they read, and news they consume. Sometimes even our family and closest friends act as sowers of the seeds of negativity.

Most people have little idea the damaging effects that such invasive thought-plants have on their attitudes and do not realize that in allowing all these poisonous seeds to be scattered into their minds, they are surrendering the autonomy and freedom of their own thinking—which in time, means their own lives and destinies.

The Impact of Attitude

Achievement-oriented people will not associate for long with someone who dwells on the negative voice. Those who listen to their negative voice attract other negative people, and those who choose to listen to their positive voice attract other positively-minded people. And this is a powerful thing because it is ultimately the people you attract to yourself who tip the scale in favor of your success or your failure.

Earlier, I said that the events of your life are not as important as how you interpret those events. But there is even more to it than that because cultivating a positive attitude will in time have an impact not only on how you see the events that unfold before you, but also on what those events are. In other words, a powerful attitude doesn't just change how you *experience* your life; it changes the *course* of that life.

As the wise mentor Pindar tells his protégé Joe in the book *The Go-Giver*:

> You'd be amazed at just how much *you* have to do with what happens *to* you.

Chuck Swindoll, one of the most influential preachers of the twentieth century, put it this way:

> The longer I live, the more I realize the impact of attitude on life. It is more important than the past, than education, than money, than circumstances, than failures, than successes, than what other people think or say or do. It is more important than appearance, giftedness, or skill. It will make or break a company, a church, a home.
>
> We cannot change our past. We cannot change the fact that people will act in a certain way. We cannot change the inevitable. The only thing we can do is play on the one string we have, and that is our attitude.

Develop a Thankful Spirit

One of the simplest ways to reset the volume knobs on your positive and negative internal voices is to focus on your blessings. It's hard to maintain a negative attitude when viewing your life through the lens of thankfulness—and just as hard to stay positive when looking through the lens of *unthankfulness*.

Thankfulness is a matter of perspective. An Indian proverb illustrates this beautifully:

> I complained that I had no shoes,
> Until I met a man who had no feet.

Resolve that you will refuse to fall into bitterness and resentment, regardless of your circumstances. Instead, choose to find and focus on the blessings in life, which are present always and everywhere, even in the darkest of times.

In *The Speaker's Quote Book*, Roy B. Zuck relates a story of a blind ninety-two-year-old woman who had recently moved to a nursing home after the death of her husband:

After many hours of waiting patiently in the lobby of the nursing home, she smiled sweetly when told her room was ready. As she maneuvered her walker to the elevator, I provided a visual description of her tiny room, including the eyelet curtains that had been hung on her window.

"I love it," she stated with the enthusiasm of an eight-year-old having just been presented with a new puppy.

"Mrs. Jones, you haven't seen the room—just wait."

"That doesn't have anything to do with it," she replied. "Happiness is something you decide on ahead of time. Whether I like the room or not doesn't depend on how the furniture is arranged. It's how I arrange my mind. I already *decided* to love it."

ALIGNMENT
"I resolve to align my subconscious mind with my conscious intention."

I learned this, at least, by my experiment: that if one advances confidently in the direction of his dreams, and endeavors to live the life which he has imagined, he will meet with a success unexpected in common hours.
— Henry David Thoreau

In the opening pages of *Walden; or, Life in the Woods*, Henry David Thoreau offers this observation of society:

The mass of men lead lives of quiet desperation.

He goes on to say that his purpose in writing this meditation on society and self-sufficiency is to learn what life had to teach him "and not, when [he] came to die, discover that [he] had not lived."

What a tragic thing: to reach the end of our days and discover that we have not truly lived at all—that we have only measured out lives of quiet desperation.

Few ever accomplish what they truly want; instead, most quietly resign themselves to their fate. Why is that? Why don't more people lead lives of triumph? Why do they not, as Thoreau prescribes in *Walden*'s conclusion, advance confidently in the direction of their dreams?

A big part of the answer has to do with a disagreement most people experience within their brains.

The Power of Dreams

Science has long recognized two distinct, contrasting aspects to the human mind. In times of antiquity, they were described by such terms as the *awake state* and *dreaming state*.

Thousands of years before Freud, humanity acknowledged the power of our dreams and understood their often prophetic nature. From biblical times on, people have understood that in some mysterious way, dreams have the capacity to predict and influence the realities of our waking lives.

William Shakespeare evoked this sense in the closing lines of *The Tempest*:

We are such stuff
As dreams are made on, and our little life
Is rounded with a sleep.

Another term for the dreaming state is *imagination*. Albert Einstein, one of the greatest minds of the twentieth century, understood well the power of imagination:

Imagination is everything. It is the preview of life's coming attractions....Imagination is more important than knowledge.

So did Napoleon, who penned this entry in his diary:

Imagination rules the world. The defect of our modern institutions is that they do not speak to the imagination.

Today, achievers in every field are taught to harness the power of the dreaming state using their imagination to visualize successful outcomes before making them a reality. From athletes to salespeople and musicians to business owners, top performers understand the power of visualization for goal achievement.

When Martin Luther King stood at the Washington Mall and addressed the gathered crowd, he did not say, "I have a plan." He understood that while a plan or strategy may make sound, logical sense, a dream has more power.

As it turns out, it has *two million times* more power.

Ant and Elephant

These days, we refer to these two aspects of the mind as our *conscious* and *subconscious* minds.

In *The Success Principles*, Jack Canfield offers this simple but profound insight:

> You only have control over three things in your life—the thoughts you think, the images you visualize, and the actions you take.

This is a brilliant summation of the anatomy of achievement. *Thoughts* are the currency of the conscious mind, while *images* are the language of the subconscious, and it is the interplay between these two that produces everything you do—your *actions*.

However, this is not an interplay of two equals because your subconscious mind is far, *far* more powerful than your conscious mind.

In *The Ant and the Elephant*, author and Olympic speed skater Vince Poscente quantifies the difference between the capacities of the conscious and subconscious mind. In the course of one second of thinking, the conscious brain stimulates two thousand neurons, and the subconscious brain stimulates *four billion* neurons. Four billion to two thousand—that's *two million* times more subconscious than conscious activities, comparable to the difference in size and weight between an elephant and…you guessed it, an ant.

Because of this, the images formed in your subconscious mind have an overwhelmingly greater influence in shaping the vision that guides your every act. The subconscious, not the conscious mind, is the mind's prime mover—by a factor of two million to one.

Now, the ant is no weakling. Ants are one of nature's most industrious creatures. Your conscious mind is terrific at formulating a plan and *initiating* a path of action. But no matter how great the plan or how much you want to see it through, you'll never stick to it for long without the staying power of the elephant.

A Civil War in Your Brain

Karl Wallenda, the world-renowned aerial acrobat who founded the Flying Wallendas, dazzled the world with his daredevil stunts. In 1978, Wallenda planned to traverse a wire stretched more than 120 feet above the pavement between two hotel towers in Puerto Rico. Although he had been performing in public for more than fifty years and was arguably the world's most accomplished high-wire artist, Wallenda was deeply worried about this feat. As his wife recalls:

> All Karl thought about for three straight months prior to it was falling. It was the first time he'd ever thought about that, and it seemed to me that he put all his energies into not falling rather than walking the tightrope.

According to Mrs. Wallenda, Karl made it a point, contrary to his usual custom, to personally supervise the installation of the tightrope and guide wires. Feeding images of disaster into his subconscious mind, he allowed his focus to become divided between his conscious intention to cross successfully and his subconscious fear of failure—and thus initiated a civil war in his mind.

Karl was the best in his craft, but even his half-century of training was no match for the power of the elephant. Tragically, when the winds rose to more than 30 mph, he lost his balance and plunged to his death.

As much as we like to think that we are in charge of our lives, the function we think of as "us"—that is, our rational, conscious mind—actually has very limited power compared with the vast resources of the elephant of our subconscious.

French psychologist Émile Coué coined what he called "the law of reversed effort," which says that the harder we try to do something by force of conscious will, the less successful we are. Coué added:

> Internal conflict occurs between the will and imagination, but the imagination is always stronger.... Every time the will and imagination come into conflict, not only can we not do that which we wish, but we do precisely the contrary.

As much as we want, hope, and even believe that our ant can prevail, it doesn't stand a chance. Coué's observations echo the poignant words of the Apostle Paul in his *Epistle to the Romans* (Romans 7:15, NIV):

> I do not understand what I do. For what I want to do, I do not do, but what I hate, I do.

It was this constant frustration of conscious intentions gone awry that the poet Robert Burns mourned in his famous couplet:

> The best-laid schemes o' mice an' men
> Gang aft agley [often go awry],

An' lea'e [leave] us nought but grief and pain,
For promised joy!

The soaring eloquence of Burns and the Apostle Paul,
and even the modern dieter's lament ("Why can't I seem to
stick with the program?"), serve as expressions of the sad
casualties that invariably result from the civil war in our
minds, the war between ant and elephant.

If dreams are compelling visions of the future, then
worries are *fearful* visions of the future. And on the question
of success or failure, imagination is neutral. It is simply an
obedient elephant, applying its massive strength to bring
about whatever prevailing images it has been fed.

Your elephant is always charging, every second of every
hour of your life. The only question is: Is it carrying you
toward your dreams, or toward your fears?

Who Is Feeding Your Elephant?

Just as you are the gardener of your mind, the one with
ultimate say over what seeds are planted there, you are
also the zookeeper of both ant and elephant. You are in
charge of what they are fed.

Unfortunately, just as many allow trespassers to scatter
weeds into the gardens of their minds, many also give up
the care and feeding of their subconscious minds—their
elephants—to others.

Your elephant is always feeding on something. And if
you don't feed it, someone else will—someone, for example,
like those in the television industry.

According to the latest research, the average American
watches more than five hours of television every day—and
television advertisers are highly skilled at speaking to the
elephant in your head. They have learned to skip right past
the ant mind and instead use carefully crafted images that
speak directly to the subconscious, replacing the viewer's
imagination with images of the advertisers' own design.

Because of this, people end up buying things that they don't really need based on emotion rather than rationally understanding why they did it. Advertisers have literally programmed their minds.

For example, can you imagine a beer commercial that explains the ratio of carbonated water to barley and hops? Or an ad that features a beer producer speaking directly to the viewer and saying, "Our beer tastes pretty much like most beers, but it will dull your frontal lobe and slightly relax your inhibitions, enabling you to act silly without embarrassment...of course, it will also impair your judgment. But we hope you'll weigh the risks and decide to buy some"? Not likely!

What do you see instead? You see images of a guy popping open a tall cold one and then beautiful bikini-clad women appearing out of nowhere and fawning all over him.

Rationally, everyone watching knows this isn't going to happen—that is, everyone knows that *consciously*. But in the target audience—men, especially aged eighteen to whatever—the elephant mind thrums to the image like a plucked guitar string...and then charges out to buy the beer.

There is an old saying in sales: People make purchase decisions emotionally and then justify them rationally. The elephant does the buying and leaves it to the ant to explain.

Psychologist Timothy Wilson, author of *Strangers to Ourselves*, writes:

> The adaptive unconscious plays a major executive role in our mental lives. It gathers information, interprets and evaluates it, and sets goals in motion, quickly and efficiently.

The images fed to your elephant become your reality. And unlike the conscious mind, the subconscious never sleeps. It is performing its millions of neural functions every second of every minute of every hour, around the clock, now and for the rest of your life.

Make no mistake; the elephant mind *will* be fed. But *who* is feeding it? And *what* is it being fed?

Aligning Ant and Elephant

When you assume responsibility for what you are feeding your elephant, you change your thoughts, and the moment that happens, you change your destiny.

In his classic *The Magic of Believing*, Claude M. Bristol writes about how to feed the elephant:

> This subtle force of repeated suggestion overcomes our reason. It acts directly on our emotions and our feelings, and finally penetrates to the very depths of our subconscious minds. It's the repeated suggestion that makes you believe.

In the same way an actor plays out what is written in a film script, we each act out our lives according to whatever is written into the script of our subconscious minds.

In order to "advance confidently in the direction of your dreams," you have to feed your subconscious a script that will point it in that direction. Olympic gymnast Peter Vidmar stresses this point:

> Visualization is not a substitute for hard work and dedication. But if you add it to your training regimen—whether in sports, business, or your personal relationships—you will prepare your mind for success, which is the first step in achieving all your goals and dreams.

In *Engineering and the Mind's Eye*, Eugene Ferguson writes:

> Pyramids, cathedrals, and rockets exist not because of geometry, theory of structures, or thermodynam-

ics, but because they were first pictures—literally visions—in the minds of those who first conceived them.

Don't misunderstand the point; this isn't some magical elixir but rather a logical plan to utilize the entire brain for goal achievement. It will still take effort and drive to achieve your aims—but by aligning the ant of your conscious intentions with the images you are feeding to the elephant of your subconscious, you bring the civil war inside your mind to a peaceful conclusion and lay the foundation for massive results.

A few years ago, the U.S. Navy SEAL sniper training course implemented a program of visualization and mental rehearsal based on the work of Olympic shooter Lanny Bassham, author of *With Winning in Mind*. As SEAL sniper instructor Brandon Webb recalls:

> The first time I started teaching the mental management material as part of our course, some of the students were as skeptical as I had been at first.... When that class's first shooting test came up, [the two snipers who had used the material] both shot perfect 100s. We had *never* had a pair shoot perfect 100s. It was the highest score in U.S. Navy SEAL sniper course history.

Nearly every world-class athlete has learned the secret of aligning the ant and the elephant, and it is just as effective in other fields.

In 1987, a struggling actor, barely able to pay his bills, drove his old Toyota up Mulholland Drive into the Hollywood Hills. As he stared down at the lights of the City of Angels, he declared an armistice in his internal civil war. He wrote himself a check for $10 million, dated the check for Thanksgiving 1995—then eight years in the future—and wrote on the memo line, "For acting services rendered."

At the time, it was rare for even the most successful A-list actors to earn such an outlandish amount. And a complete unknown? Ridiculous! Still, the young man knew what he was doing: He was aligning his ant with his elephant. When his conscious mind wrote that $10 million check, he was purposefully feeding his subconscious mind a vision of his future reality.

By Thanksgiving of 1995, Jim Carrey was able to cash that check, and today he routinely earns well more than double that amount for his "acting services rendered."

People will discipline their conscious mind to make a living, but few will discipline their subconscious mind to achieve their dreams. However, those who do go on to accomplish extraordinary things—as Thoreau put it, they "meet with a success unexpected in common hours."

PRACTICE
"I resolve to develop and implement a game plan in each area of my life."

Theory without practice is futile;
practice without theory is fatal.
— Confucius

Many years ago, while working as an engineer at General Motors at the tender age of twenty-four, I learned about the power of the planning process from the great William Edwards Deming, the father of the modern quality control movement.

One day, Dr. Deming came to speak at a GM conference on the topic of statistical controls. What I learned that day revolutionized the way I pursue goals.

Dr. Deming talked to us about the practice of using experiments as tests to determine the accuracy of our predictions. "If our thinking is correct," he said, "then we should be able to predict the results of the experiment. But if the results do not come out as predicted, then the original thinking was not fully accurate and would require changing and then retesting."

He called his methodology PDCA—plan, do, check, and act—known today as the Deming Cycle.

Plan, Do, Check, Adjust

As I listened to Deming, I realized that his PDCA process could be applied not only to engineering, but to anything. Altering Deming's wording slightly to make it "plan, do, check, and *adjust*," I started using this approach in as many areas of my life as I could.

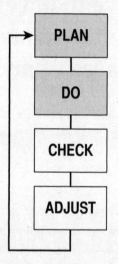

I soon came to view life as an ongoing test—an opportunity to predict results based on planned behaviors, test those predictions in real time, and determine whether my predictions had been accurate or needed some adjustments.

Having a game plan is *necessary* but not *sufficient*. To achieve your intended outcome, you need to formulate a game plan and then implement it, check it, and adjust it based on what you learn from whatever gap there is between your plan and your actual results—and then repeat the cycle, closing the gap until the game plan works perfectly.

Simply put, in order to achieve your aims, you must *plan your work and work your plan.*

The PDCA process allows you to sort fact from fiction in any area of your life. It ensures that your predictions are accurate and not just assumptions—for assumptions are the facts of fools, and fools soon join the ranks of failures.

The Magic of Doing

Q: Five frogs sat on a lily pad; one decided to jump off. How many were left?

A: All five—that one frog only *decided* to jump. It didn't actually *do* it yet.

If the road to hell is paved with good intentions, then that road must be very thickly paved. Every politician has a plan; few exercise the will to execute them.

The PDCA process depends squarely on the game plan you create—but the best plan in the world is worthless unless you implement it. As Confucius pointed out, the journey of a thousand miles begins with the first step. That's the first *step*—not simply holding the map. Greatness begins when you marshal the courage to act on your plan.

For example, let's say you want to become proficient as a public speaker. Part of the PLAN step is to honestly review areas where you can potentially improve. Asking the right questions is crucial to good planning. What's the difference between good speakers and poor speakers? Where are you currently strong, and what are your current weaknesses? What sort of game plan would help you make the improvements you need to shore up those areas and become more proficient as a speaker?

Then once you have identified those areas where you could improve, it's time to *start speaking*.

You cannot improve your craft unless you *perform*, over and over, even if you have to make mistake after mistake until you become proficient. There simply is no substitute. Anyone who is unwilling to first look bad will never become good.

Deliberate Practice

"I am a great believer in luck. The harder I work, the more of it I seem to have." This quote has been attributed to Thomas Jefferson, the legendary film producer Sam Goldwyn, and others. Whoever first said it deserves a medal.

In chapter 1, I mentioned what Malcolm Gladwell calls the 10,000-Hour Rule: It takes about 10,000 hours of diligent practice to achieve mastery in anything. The reason successful people appear "lucky" to others is that most people are not aware of that 10,000 hours. Those years of committed effort are like the bulk of a great iceberg lying unseen below the water's surface. People see the results but cannot fathom what produced them...so they call it "luck." But no one lucks into long-term success. Luck is a loser's excuse for a winner's commitment.

In his book *Talent Is Overrated*, Geoff Colvin explains that all high achievers go through a process called *deliberate practice*:

> Deliberate practice is characterized by several elements, each worth examining. It is activity designed specifically to improve performance, often with a teacher's help; it can be repeated a lot; feedback on results is continuously available; it's highly demanding mentally, whether the activity is purely intellectual, such as chess or business-related activities, or heavily physical, such as sports; and it isn't much fun.

Deliberate practice, which is simply another name for PDCA, is what separates the amateurs from the professionals in any field. Amateurs practice skills they are comfortable with, while professionals push at the limits of their skills in an effort to move past their current competence. Only by pushing past your comfort zone can you hope to improve your current competence.

Abraham Lincoln invested his 10,000 hours of deliberate practice in personal development and the art of interacting with people, commenting, "I will work, I will study, and when my moment comes, I will be ready." Amidst many years of trials and tribulations, Lincoln deliberately pursued a rigorous practice of the PDCA process.

Colvin discusses the importance of pushing past the comfort zone in deliberate practice:

> Great performers never allow themselves to reach the automatic, arrested-development stage in their chosen field. That is the effect of continual deliberate practice—avoiding automaticity. The essence of practice, which is constantly trying to do the things one cannot do comfortably, makes automatic behavior impossible....Avoiding automaticity through continual practice is another way of saying that great performers are always getting better.

Nobody "lucks into" success at the level of mastery— unless we use the word "luck" as an acronym for *Laboring Under Correct Knowledge*.

Make Your Work a Game

While there is no shortcut past the 10,000 hours it takes to achieve mastery in any field, there *is* a shortcut through the monotony of it: make it into a game.

Mark Twain provides a memorable example: This is exactly how Tom Sawyer maneuvers his friends into helping him whitewash a fence he was assigned to do as punishment. He makes it look like he is having the time of his life, and soon they all plead to join him.

When work becomes a game, the tasks of work turn into the plays of the game. You don't even realize you are working because you enjoy the tasks as part of advancing in the game.

Consider a man on a hot autumn day having to choose between playing tennis and raking the lawn. He could happily stay on the court and play for hours, pushing himself to his limit. Yet he looks at the rake with dread, procrastinating as long as possible—even though it would take no more effort to rake the lawn than it would to play tennis.

Both require effort and discipline; both are exhausting. What's the difference? He perceives one as a game and the other as work.

When you come to view your work as a game, you no longer do *tasks*—instead, you are playing a game, and playing to win. As *Swim with the Sharks (Without Being Eaten Alive)* author Harvey MacKay puts it:

> Find something you love to do, and you'll never work a day in your life.

All top performers have learned to do this in their fields of mastery, whether in business, sports, or music. Work isn't simply work anymore; rather, it is part of the process to win the game that they love.

Highly successful people have tapped into this reservoir of energy by creating a game out of their professions, thus falling in love with the process and the quest for excellence in order to win. Imagine how productive everyone would be if they worked their professions as hard as they work their hobbies. Better still, imagine the purpose-filled work that would happen if everyone's professions were their passions.

Quitters, Campers, and Climbers

Paul Stoltz, author of *Adversity Quotient*, describes three types of people: *quitters*, *campers*, and *climbers*.

All three begin life in the valley staring up at the mountain of potential accomplishment. Yet despite the fact that every one of us is born with the impulse to climb, the mountaintop remains practically empty.

There are billions of people in the world. What happened to everyone else?

1) Quitters

Life's quitters see the mountain's jagged cliffs, threatening storms, and endless paths as dangerous. Unwilling to endure the difficulties, disappointments, and persistent repetition that are its price, they choose to pass on the climb entirely and stay put where they are.

Quitters are typically people who entertain themselves into oblivion, escaping into drugs, sex, or other time-consuming activities that make scant positive contribution to the world, or none at all. They keep themselves busy doing mindless activities in order to avoid the pain of the mountain. Yet in the long run, they suffer the worst pain of all—the pain of regret.

By denying their God-given urge to climb, quitters endure only by making major compromises in their lives. Sadly, they comprise the majority of humanity.

2) Campers

Campers look up at the mountain and start climbing, using some version of the PDCA process. Excited about the opportunities ahead, they begin the ascent with enthusiasm. But at some point along the way, they stop, lulled into complacency by the partial achievements of their lifestyle.

They may achieve a decent view partway up the mountainside, but they have compromised their ideals and sold out their courage for the comfort of the plateau and the safety it seems to offer. They may convince themselves they are only resting for a season, but few will ever break camp and resume the climb.

They have *settled*, and their best days are behind them. Whether or not they realize it, they have traded in their dreams for the rewards of mediocrity.

Some of the most talented people fall into this camp, hypnotizing themselves into believing that their lifestyle is more important than their purpose.

Don't misread this; everyone needs a pause in the action, a vacation once in a while to refresh—but not a vacation from the rest of life. Take a break when needed, but never compromise your calling for your comforts. Vacations end—but your purpose? Never.

3) Climbers

Climbers are those few brave souls who choose to press on with the PDCA process as far as they can go, no matter how difficult or painful the climb. They know they were called to scale the mountain and will do whatever it takes to accomplish it.

Climbers are a rare breed. They never sacrifice their convictions for convenience. They understand that life is not about obtaining the best spot in camp or gathering the most items in the tent. Life isn't about possessions, but about purpose; it's about the climb.

A climber is someone who has learned that one of the keys to a happy life is fulfilling one's purpose, becoming who he is intended to be, not necessarily by reaching the top, but through the constant effort to improve.

A true climber battles his mountain, and in the process, he conquers himself. His climb leaves a path for others to follow in pursuit of their purpose and dreams, teaching other climbers the lessons he has learned through life's mountain climb.

Each of us must make our own decision as we gaze up at the mountain of life. Will we quit, camp, or climb?

The Price of Success

There are three simple steps to success:

1. What do you want?
2. What does it cost?
3. Pay it.

You may be thinking, *It can't be that simple!* But it *is* that simple. It's just not easy. In fact, each step gets progressively harder.

Many people—though fewer than you might think—can readily identify what they want. Far fewer ever grasp the nature and extent of the commitment it will take to achieve that—the cost. And only a rare few will move through those steps and on to the third, which is to actually *do* what is involved in paying that price.

This is because you can't pay for success by just writing a check—and you certainly can't put it on a charge card! The price of success comes with its own terms, and it is not a lump sum. It can only be paid over time, in daily installments. Only after every installment plus interest has been paid in full will one receive the prize.

This is why success is not for the weak of heart: There is a certain amount of pain involved because rigorously revealing the shortcomings in your thinking can be a painful experience. In fact, one of the biggest drivers that allows a person to endure the pain of deliberate practice is the criticism of others. Winners turn rejection into productive energy, as psychologist Henry Link describes in his book *The Rediscovery of Man*:

> A sense of inferiority, we find is not a disease. I have told hundreds of complaining parents: You should be thankful that your child has a sense of inferiority. The children to worry about are those who always think they are smart, who know better than

their elders, who see no reason for painful practice or humble effort.

As American philosopher Robert Grudin explains in *The Grace of Great Things*:

> Individuals who spend their lives in the persistent avoidance of pain are not likely to amount to much....
> Mastery demands endless practice of technical operations, endless assaults on seemingly ineluctable concepts, humiliation by teachers, anxious and exhausting competition with peers. To gain such mastery, one must face the sting of pertinent criticism, the shock of a thousand minor failures, and the nagging fear of one's own unimprovable inadequacy....
> A tiny minority gets through to the top, to memorable excellence or profound understanding. The rest of us stop along the way, perhaps for a temporary rest, perhaps for a period of reassessment. But once we stop, we are unlikely to start up again.

Dreams become plans, and what you do with those plans dictates whether your dreams will become realities or remain insubstantial fantasies.

Develop a game plan for success in every area of your life, put it into action, and then evaluate your results with unflinching honesty.

RESOLUTION 6

SCORE
"I resolve to keep score
in the game of life."

Trust, but verify.
— Ronald Reagan

The pilot climbs into the cockpit of the F/A-18 Hornet preparing to explode off the aircraft carrier's deck in hot pursuit of his mission at a staggering velocity of close to twice the speed of sound.

"Charlie Fox Trot," comes the voice from Ground Control over his earpiece, "proceed with systems check. Over."

The pilot keys his mike and replies, "Nah, Ground Base, think I'll skip the systems check today...everything checked out okay on Thursday, the last time I went up, so I'm pretty much good to go—" and he blasts off into the sky....

Ridiculous, right? Of course it is. But it happens all the time. No, not with fighter pilots, but with the people around us every day as they climb into the cockpits of their lives.

If you happen to be a fighter pilot—or a NASCAR driver, or a mountain climber heading for Everest or K2—then you are one of those rare individuals who is well acquainted with steps 3 and 4 of the PDCA process. In fact, your life quite literally depends on it.

But what about the rest of us who do not face life-threatening challenges in our everyday lives?

Our lives depend on it, too. If we skip over the CHECK step, it may not kill us today, or tomorrow, or even next week. But we are headed for failure as sure as our fictional fighter pilot is headed for trouble. We may not *lose* our lives, but we will fail to *live* them as the fulfilled, purposeful lives of excellence they were meant to be.

The Critical Step

Many people execute some variation of the first step of the PDCA process, even if they don't call it that. Of all those who *plan*, fewer take the second step and actually *do* what they thought about doing. But even among those who both plan *and* do, very few complete the process with the CHECK and ADJUST steps.

In fact, the great majority of people resist step 3, the CHECK step, with everything they've got.

Why is that? Because this step requires brutal honesty.

Step 3 is when our defense mechanisms kick in, in an effort to protect our fragile egos from the revelation of the truth about our current performance. It can be embarrassing to discover the gap between the skills we want and the skills we have. Most people would rather delude themselves and be happy than confront themselves and exert the effort to improve.

But running or hiding from the data doesn't change anything. An ostrich may stick its head in the sand to avoid its fear of lions—but sadly, that has no bearing on the lion's dinner plans.

The point of the PLAN and DO steps is not simply to do for the sake of doing, but to *learn*, and the learning doesn't happen unless and until you proceed on to step 3.

The CHECK step encompasses the act of self-reflection, the capacity to look at ourselves with unflinching objectivity and face the truth of our actual results—not our hoped-for, intended, or perceived results.

For most people, this is very difficult. But that is why working on *this* step is often what will make the greatest difference in our personal growth.

Keeping Score

In chapter 1, we envisioned a basketball game without a net. Now imagine you have a net—but no scoreboard! How can you tell how you're doing, or if you are advancing at all? You can't.

The CHECK step is life's scoreboard. Without a scoreboard, you simply cannot identify the areas where you need to improve.

A good coach studies the data during the halftime break to determine why his team is winning or losing and makes the necessary adjustments based on what the scoreboard reveals in order to achieve victory. In the same way, the CHECK step provides the scoreboard that tells you whether or not the strategies you are employing are moving you toward your personal and professional objectives.

In comparing great companies to merely good companies, Jim Collins discovered that their relationship to the CHECK step was a critical factor:

> The great companies continually refined the path to greatness with the brutal facts of reality.

The comparison companies in his study, on the other hand, did not.

Note that simply *gathering* information is not enough. Unless you use the gathered data as a critical scoreboard and confront what it is truly saying, the windows to greatness will remain shuttered to you. In fact, Collins writes:

> We found no evidence that the good-to-great companies had more or better information than the com-

parison companies. None. Both sets of companies had virtually identical access to good information. The key, then, lies not in better information, but in turning information into information that cannot be ignored.

Finding Gold in the Bad News

Yes, many people resist step 3. But it's not that these people don't do any kind of check or review of their results. They do. They just don't tell the truth about what they see.

The temptation is to downplay bad news, put a happy face on the findings, or fudge the data—anything to avoid facing the truth. Governments do this, corporations do this, organizations do this, and individuals do this. But it is a sure path to ruin.

Those on the path to greatness understand that bad news *cannot* be downplayed, but must be confronted head on and right away. That is the only way to identify accurately those areas where improvement is possible. Indeed, people on the path to mastery actively *seek out* bad news, knowing that it contains the seeds of success.

In *Direct from Dell*, Michael Dell writes:

It was clear that in 1993 we didn't have the information we needed to run our business. We didn't fully understand the relationship between costs, revenues, and profits within the different parts of our business. There were internal disagreements about which businesses were worthwhile and which were not. We were making decisions based on emotions and opinions.

In leadership, it's important to be intuitive, but not at the expense of facts. Without the right data to back it up, emotion-based decision-making during difficult times will inevitably lead a company into greater danger. That's precisely what was happening to us.

At the time, Dell was being deceived by rumors and conflicting opinions. Only after developing a working scoreboard was he able to sort out fact from fiction and start dealing with reality.

Dell confronted his business's brutal reality and thereby gained a multibillion-dollar competitive advantage while in his twenties.

There's Always Room for Adjustment

Once you have checked the results of your actions and identified the gaps between your intended objectives and the actual results, it's time to make the adjustments that will help you close that gap and proceed further up the mountain.

But what if you don't need to? What if your data tells you that you're doing pretty well? Then you can skip that last step, right?

Wrong. As crucial as it is to learn from failure, it is equally vital to develop the habit of learning from your apparent successes as well. Finding the lessons in failure keeps you *hopeful*, and finding the lessons in victory keeps you *humble*. Finding a victory in every defeat and a defeat in every victory is the secret to keeping both hopelessness and pride at bay. There never has been and never will be a perfect performance.

When you confront bad news, as Michael Dell did in the nineties, the opportunity for improvement is obvious. But be careful; it is when the CHECK step brings you good news that you are most vulnerable—because it's so easy to get complacent.

When your data says you've done well, put your ego in check and dig deeper.

People on the path to mastery are never content with merely good performance, but are always seeking clues to the elusive greatness that lies ahead.

Don't get me wrong: I'm not saying you should not enjoy your successes. Celebrate them! But don't let them lull you into neglecting the all-important CHECK and ADJUST steps of the cycle of constant improvement.

Unless you learn to sacrifice your ego on the altar of truth, you will sacrifice the truth on the altar of your ego.

Three Ways People Avoid Keeping Score

Here are three common ways people avoid confronting the reality of the scoreboard.

1) Pass the Buck

When hoped-for results fail to materialize, it is tempting to cast blame elsewhere. In that case, who loses? The person doing the blaming loses.

Anytime you ascribe your own lack of results to factors outside yourself—poor mentorship, lazy teammates, unsupportive spouses, the economy—you surrender control of your life to circumstances.

Winners refuse to pass the buck, knowing that if they do, they will release the tension created by the pain of losing—and that it is this tension that generates the motivation to change.

Don't fall for the seductive blame game. The amount of time you spend pointing fingers at anything or anyone outside yourself is the amount of time you are investing in your future failure. Work on better skills, not better excuses. Search for ways to be responsible. You can make a million dollars or a million excuses, but not both.

If you don't own your losses, you cannot own any victories.

Lou Holtz, former head coach at the University of Notre Dame, writes in *Wins, Losses, and Lessons*:

The person who has never made a mistake in his own mind, who obfuscates and attempts to deflect blame, is someone you should approach cautiously. I've fouled up plenty in my life. In most circumstances, I've done my best to own up to my mistakes and take whatever steps I could to correct them.

Is it any surprise that he won a national championship, led six different universities to bowl games, and was elected to the College Football Hall of Fame?

2) Decide It's Not Worth It

"When the going gets tough..." (yes, you know how that one ends) "...the tough get going." But here's what also happens: "...the majority decide it wasn't really worth it anyway."

Oh, they may not *say* that—not those literal words. The resignation of quitting is often disguised with such phrases as, "Things are pretty good as they are," or, "I'm doing pretty well," or, "This is not so bad."

This is a tragic mistake. The error lies in thinking that if, instead of pressing on to the top of the mountain, one settles for a nice location halfway up the slope, one should be able to experience, well, at least *half* the happiness and fulfillment. Makes sense, right?

But it doesn't work that way. Success is not an arithmetic problem. The error is this: Success is not the destination, but the journey. It is not reaching the mountaintop that matters, but the striving for it. Once you let go of the climb, you let go of your purpose—and then there is no alternative but to slide ever downward.

When sharpshooter Lanny Bassham went to his first Olympics in 1972, he was confident he would take the gold in his event. But he didn't. At the last minute, he choked and came in second place. Back in the States, he went to see as many sports psychologists as he could to help him understand why he had choked. They all told him, "Hey, it's okay to be number two. Olympic silver is a great achievement, Lanny; you should be satisfied with that."

Lanny said, "I don't think so!" He used that failure to create what became a revolutionary approach to mental management that is used worldwide today. And when he returned to the Olympics in 1976, he took the gold.

3) Settle for Vicarious Victories

Because we are hardwired to keep score, it is virtually impossible to completely surrender the urge to compete. Therefore, human beings throughout history have used a very clever mechanism for letting themselves off the hook of greatness and genuine fulfillment, while still satisfying the biological imperative of the scoreboard.

How have they done this? By transferring their innate sense of competition from themselves onto others, seeking to pursue excellence vicariously through others' achievements. Some of these people are called *sports fans*. Fans feel the thrill of victory and the agony of defeat with absolutely no growth of their own required.

Don't misunderstand; I am not criticizing professional sports or the teams who play them—far from it. They are superb examples of PDCA. Show me an accomplished athlete in any sport, and I'll show you someone who practices the PLAN, DO, CHECK, and ADJUST steps like a religion.

My point is that the opportunity for excellence is every bit as available to everyone sitting in the stands as it is to those on the field.

The Stockdale Paradox

How is it possible to confront the brutal facts, both personally and professionally, without losing confidence in an eventual victory? Jim Collins writes:

In every case, the management team responded with a powerful psychological duality. On the one hand, they stoically accepted the brutal facts of reality. On the other hand, they maintained an unwavering faith in the endgame, and a commitment to prevail as a great company despite the brutal facts.

Collins and his team dubbed this dual capacity for brutal honesty and absolute faith the Stockdale Paradox, after Vice Admiral James Stockdale, who went through seven years of captivity in Vietnam, during which he was routinely beaten and tortured. When interviewed by Collins, Stockdale said that even though he was never given an ounce of hope that he would ever be released, he refused to lose faith:

> I never doubted not only that I would get out, but also that I would prevail in the end and turn the experience into the defining event of my life, which, in retrospect, I would not trade.

When Collins asked him about those prisoners who did not make it out alive, Stockdale replied:

> That's easy: the optimists. They were the ones who said, "We're going to be out by Christmas." And Christmas would come, and Christmas would go. Then they'd say, "We're going to be out by Easter." And Easter would come, and Easter would go. And then Thanksgiving, and then it would be Christmas again—and they died of a broken heart.

Faith and optimism are not the same thing. Pure optimists fail to assess their situation truthfully, building false hopes that leave them vulnerable and defenseless before harsh realities.

Like Stockdale, great companies and great individuals consistently confront facts and refuse to give in to denial, complacency, or blind optimism. Regardless of the current score, they maintain an unwavering belief that they will overcome and win, no matter how difficult or painful the change process may be.

The Point of Perfection

After completing the ADJUST step, what's next? It's time to start the cycle again from step 1, making new plans and preparing for their execution.

The best in any field repeat the PDCA cycle continuously as they steadily gain mastery of their craft—and of themselves. The goal is to improve both personally and professionally, closing the gap between where one is and where one desires to be.

The point, as the Lexus slogan puts it, is "the relentless pursuit of perfection."

Success is for the few—but not the "talented few." Talent has nothing to do with it. No, success is for the *courageous* few who are willing to face the truth about themselves so they may continue to grow and improve.

Be patient with the PDCA process. Most people overestimate the amount of change they can achieve in a year and underestimate the amount that can occur over ten years. Rome was not built in a day and oak trees do not mature overnight.

Success will take time—and be all the sweeter for it.

FRIENDSHIP
"I resolve to practice the art and science of friendship."

Un pour tous, tous pour un!
(One for all, all for one!)
— Alexandre Dumas in *The Three Musketeers*

The Ancient Greeks had four distinct words that communicated different perspectives on the concept of love: *agape*, *eros*, *storge*, and *philia*. *Agape* embodies sacrificial love; *eros* describes sensual love; *storge* is the affection of family ties; and *philia* is the kind of love that gives Philadelphia both its name [from the Greek *philos* (loving) and *adelphos* (brother)] and its nickname: *The City of Brotherly Love.*

Aristotle described *philia* as loyalty to friends, family, and community requiring virtue, equality, and familiarity. It is best represented by the love shared between two longtime close friends.

It is this last type of love that is the focus of this resolution.

Eight Principles of True Friendship

There are indications that this type of friendship is on the decline today. A 2006 study published in the *American*

Sociological Review showed that between 1985 and 2004, the average number of people with whom respondents said they could "discuss matters of importance" had dropped by nearly one-third, and the number of those who said they had no close confidants at all more than doubled, from one in eight to one in four.

Apparently this decline is not unique to our generation. Writing half a century ago, C. S. Lewis described a similar change in the value of friendship:

> To the Ancients, Friendship seemed the happiest and most fully human of all loves; the crown of life and the school of virtue. The modern world, in comparison, ignores it...It is something quite marginal; not a main course in life's banquet; a diversion; something that fills up the chinks of one's time.

Yet developing such friendships is critical to our happiness. As Harvard public policy professor Robert Putnam writes in his book *Bowling Alone*:

> What is the single most common finding from half a century of research on the correlates of life satisfaction?...That happiness is best predicted by the breadth and depth of one's social connections.

Through decades of being blessed with wonderful friendships, along with extensive research in the field, I have identified what to me are the eight essential principles for building and maintaining long-term *philia* friendships:

1. True friendships form around a common bond.
2. True friends accept one another despite their human imperfections.
3. True friends approve of one another.
4. True friends appreciate one another.
5. True friends listen to each other's hopes, dreams, fears, and struggles.

6. True friends celebrate one another's successes.
7. True friends are trustworthy.
8. True friends are loyal.

1) True Friendships Form around a Common Bond

True friends may begin as acquaintances or companions of circumstance, but their bond then goes further, developing into a deep love and respect for one another.

Typically the seed of this growth is some specific interest that the two discover they share in common. C. S. Lewis describes this process of discovery:

Friendship arises out of mere companionship when two or more of the companions discover that they have in common some insight or interest or even taste which the others do not share and which, till that moment, each believed to be his own unique treasure (or burden). The typical expression of opening Friendship would be something like, "What? You too? I thought I was the only one."

There is an indescribable joy in discovering and being discovered by another human being. Emerson describes this feeling:

The glory of friendship is not the outstretched hand, not the kindly smile, nor the joy of companionship; it is the spiritual inspiration that comes to one when you discover that someone believes in you and is willing to trust you with a friendship.

Aristotle distinguishes between genuine friendship and two counterfeit types—one founded on utility, the other on pleasure. A friendship based purely on utility, such as with a shopkeeper whose store you frequent, survives only as long as both parties receive benefit. A friendship rooted in a shared pleasure, as with golfing buddies, ends when one party no longer wants to engage in the activity.

The bond of genuine friendship is based on something more enduring. According to Aristotle:

> It is those who desire the good of their friends for the friends' sake that are most truly friends, because each loves the other for what he is, and not for any incidental quality.

While the bond of friendship often begins with some particular interest in common, it does not end there. The common interest itself is simply a doorway through which we discover something deeper—which is that we genuinely enjoy one another's company.

2) True Friends Accept One Another

The bonds of trust that true friends build cannot easily be unwound, especially when those bonds are infused with forgiveness and grace. Friends offer one another grace when they make mistakes, recognizing that in the future, they may need grace themselves. They see their friends' hidden hurts, fears, and vulnerabilities, and love them anyway, warts and all.

Everyone makes mistakes, but as Saint Peter wrote, "Love covers a multitude of sins" (I Peter 4:8, NLT). A friend loves his friends enough to see past their faults and foibles and recognize the talents and treasures buried within.

In *How to Have Confidence and Power in Dealing with People*, Les Giblin shares what he calls the triple-A formula for building strong relationships. The first of these three A's is acceptance.

Acceptance does not necessarily mean that you approve of everything your friend does. Acceptance means that you embrace your friend as a human being, no matter what.

Rather than glossing over your faults and failures, a true friend accepts the truth of your present reality.

People often get this backwards and think they cannot accept another until he does things "right." But no one does everything right. Everyone needs to grow, and it is only in the soil of acceptance that the soul can find the nourishment it needs to do so. Knowing that you are clearly witnessed and are loved and accepted anyway helps you to confront the facts as they are and then move closer to becoming the person you could be.

3) True Friends Approve of One Another

Approval, the second of Giblin's three A's, takes acceptance one step further, singling out specific traits or behaviors for approbation. If acceptance means *withholding condemnation*, then approval is *bestowing commendations*.

The key is not to simply point out your friend's obvious attributes, but to seek out and acknowledge lesser-known strengths that others may not have noticed.

For example, suppose a friend of yours is a professional race-car driver. Telling him he's a great driver has little value; everyone already knows that. But if you point out what a thoughtful parent he is, he'll never forget your kind words.

Sadly, these kinds of compliments are often spoken only at a person's funeral after his passing. Why wait for the funeral when doing so now could mean so much?

Become a professional observer of excellence, and share your observations generously. Just as motor oil reduces friction in an engine, the oil of approval reduces heat and friction in relationships. It also strengthens the friend's resolve to fulfill his purpose.

A *New York Times* article on friendship cites a fascinating study:

Researchers studied thirty-four students at the University of Virginia, taking them to the base of a steep hill and fitting them with a weighted backpack. They were then asked to estimate the steepness of the hill. Some participants stood next to friends during the exercise, while others were alone. The students who stood with friends gave lower estimates of the steepness of the hill. And the longer the friends had known each other, the less steep the hill appeared.

Notice that in this study, the friends were not helping to carry one another's load; they simply stood with each other and built each other's confidence. Greek philosopher Epicurus noted:

> It is not so much our friends' help that helps us as the confident knowledge that they will help us.

4) True Friends Appreciate One Another

If acceptance is the appetizer, then approval is the main dish—and appreciation, the third of Giblin's three A's, is dessert.

One of the greatest things we can do for our friends is to help them turn up the positive internal voice and tune out the negative voice. Friends help friends think better of themselves and their opportunities by pointing out the positive. This way, a true friend helps his friend win his battle of the mind by loaning him his positive belief.

Some people have a habit of dwelling on the negative and amplify that channel in those they spend time with. But true friends magnify each other's positive voice. Choose your friends wisely because you become much like those you associate with.

To truly appreciate people, share all the good you can find in them, not only directly with them but also with others. This is the noble obverse face of gossip: sharing with the world all the good things you know about your friends.

Here is one of the great mysteries of the miracle of friendship: All that you do that helps to support and honor your friend turns out to nourish you as well. Here is how Bob Burg and John David Mann put it in *Go-Givers Sell More*:

> The word *appreciate* comes from the Latin *appreti-are*, which means "to set a price to." Over the centuries it came to mean both "an expression of one's estimate of something, usually favorable" and "to rise in value."
>
> Interesting: when you appreciate people, *you appreciate*. And when you don't, you *depreciate*.
>
> You want to increase your own worth? *Appreciate*.

True friendship is one of those precious gifts that enrich the giver as well as the recipient.

5) True Friends Listen to Each Other

One of the best ways to show acceptance, approval, and appreciation is through listening. Friends give each other permission to unburden their hearts to one another and share their hurts and pains when life gets rough.

People can tell whether you are truly listening or simply going through the motions, waiting for them to pause long enough so you can add what's on *your* mind. One of the biggest compliments you can give someone is to genuinely listen to him.

In the midst of the struggles of the Civil War, Abraham Lincoln sent a telegram to Leonard Swett, a longtime friend, saying, "I need to see you." Swett accepted the president's request, packed his bags, and headed to Washington. As the distinguished Lincoln scholar Douglas L. Wilson reports:

Lincoln asked Swett to listen as he read from letters and position papers and then laid out, in his own words, various arguments both for and against issuing a policy of emancipation. Swett was an old friend and close confidant, and he was surely expecting Lincoln to say, "Now, what do you think?" But he didn't. Instead, when he finished he said, "Tell all the folks 'hello' when you get back to Bloomington, and I really thank you for coming." He asked Swett to come to Washington simply to listen.

In the process of unburdening his heart in the presence of a true friend, Lincoln was able to solidify his thinking.

Sometimes a friend may ask us for advice, but it is never wise to assume that our advice is being sought. More often than not, all that is being asked for is the empathetic ear and open heart of true friendship.

Nineteenth-century poet Dinah Maria Mulock Craik describes the joy of having a friend truly listen:

Oh, the comfort
the inexpressible comfort of feeling
safe with a person,
having neither to weigh thoughts nor measure
    words,
but pouring them all right out,
just as they are,
chaff and grain together;
certain that a faithful hand will take and sift them,
keep what is worth keeping,
and then with the breath of kindness blow the rest
    away.

6) True Friends Celebrate One Another's Successes

Friends dream together, laugh together, struggle together, lose together, win together, and celebrate each other's successes together. They are proud of each other's accomplishments without a hint of envy.

Friends are each other's biggest fans and cheerleaders, understanding that a win for one enriches them both.

Talking behind a friend's back is perfectly acceptable—as long as the words you speak are all about the friend's good qualities. When you cheer the accomplishments of a friend behind his back, it builds both of your reputations while raising the tide of the entire community.

John Maxwell shares a story from Andy Stanley about overcoming jealousy and envy concerning his good friend and fellow pastor Louie Giglio. As Stanley explains:

> Louie and I have been friends since the sixth grade....We met at youth camp under a bunk bed while seniors battled it out over our heads. Louie is just a phenomenal communicator. When I announce at our church that Louie Giglio is going to be speaking next week, they all start clapping and we have high attendance Sunday.

Stanley acknowledged that if it were not for the love and loyalty shared between them, jealousy and envy would have crept into their relationship and damaged their friendship—but both friends refused to let that happen. In fact, according to Maxwell:

> When Louie delivers a great message, Andy goes out of his way to praise him and celebrate with him. And Louie does the same with him. Andy said, "It's not enough to think it. I have to say it because that's how I cleanse my heart. Celebration is how you defeat jealousy."

7) True Friends Are Trustworthy

The *philia* relationship is possible only in a context of infallible trust based on unimpeachable honor. A friend hears, empathizes with, and protects the innermost thoughts of his friends. When a person shares his fears, struggles, ambitions, or dreams, a true friend can be counted on to listen without judging, empathize without pitying, and guide without lecturing.

Fair-weather friends enjoy sharing the sunny times, but when the winds of trouble signal the imminent arrival of life's thunderstorms, they make themselves scarce. A true friend stays with us and waits out the storms.

John Maxwell comments:

> False friends are like shadows, keeping close to us while we walk in the sunshine but leaving us when we cross into the shade, but real friends stick with us when trouble comes. As the old saying goes: in prosperity, our friends know us; in adversity, we know our friends.

If you have even a few true friends whom you can count on both in prosperity and in adversity, you may consider yourself truly blessed.

8) True Friends Are Loyal

A trusted friend is loyal to his friends when he is in front of them and, even more importantly, when they are not present to protect themselves. These words of Martin Luther King, Jr.'s are chilling in their indictment of false friendship:

> In the end, we will remember not the words of our enemies, but the silence of our friends.

Loyalty does not necessarily mean that you take a friend's side on any issue; it means your friend is your friend, right or wrong. True friends defend each other's character, honor, and reputation as far as the truth allows, while helping to resolve any issue privately and promptly.

Loyalty does not mean turning a blind eye to wrong behavior. Instead, it means that even when you see a friend doing something you cannot approve of, you do not abandon the friend. Instead, address the friend privately and promptly in an effort to point out his blind spot, praying that he will correct his course and not force you to choose between the friendship itself and violating your own principles.

Friends will let go of a friendship only with the greatest reluctance and after an all-out effort to set things right.

True friendship brings so much joy, fun, and fulfillment into our lives that it is worth every effort to cultivate, nourish, and protect it as the priceless treasure it is.

FINANCIAL INTELLIGENCE
"I resolve to practice financial intelligence."

*Make no expense but to do good to others
or yourself; i.e. waste nothing.*
— Benjamin Franklin

Before you read on, I invite you to take this brief financial quiz, courtesy of executive coach David Krueger, M.D., author of *The Secret Language of Money*:

> Respond to each of these two questions with a single number—and do this before reading the explanations that follow.
>
> 1) My current annual income is $_____.
> 2) In order to insure happiness and contentment financially, with no more money problems and worries, my annual income would need to be $_____.

Krueger describes the nearly universal results he has gotten in giving this quiz to hundreds of clients over the years:

> In more than nine out of ten cases, people's answers indicate that their annual income would need to be

about *twice the current level* for them to feel happy and free from money worries.

This means that someone who makes $50,000 a year believes it would take roughly $100,000 a year in order to be financially content, and someone who makes $500,000—five times the first person's magic number—believes that the figure would need to be about *$1 million* a year.

In other words, no matter how much or how little you earn, chances are good that you *think* you'd need about twice that amount in order to be financially secure.

The truth of the matter is that people can be wealthy or broke no matter *what* their income level. Why? Because wealth is not about what you *earn*; it is about what you *keep*.

Ten Steps to Financial Freedom

Over the years, I have developed ten steps that, when rigorously applied, will help overcome even the worst financial train wreck and allow you to regain financial control and liberty in life.

1. Quantify your net income.
2. Quantify your expenses and profit.
3. Set a financial goal.
4. Never finance anything that depreciates.
5. Set a price limit on spontaneous purchases.
6. Shift from credit to cash.
7. Wipe out all consumer debt.
8. Understand the difference between an investment and an expense.
9. Focus on quality of life and peace of mind.
10. Be a blessing to others.

Mastering the other twelve resolutions in this book *without* also mastering finances would be a futile enterprise, like pouring buckets of water into a barrel while failing to repair the gaping hole in its floor. Yes, you want to fill the barrel. But if there are holes in the bottom, you need to repair them *starting now*, or all that fine water will quickly dissipate, leaving you as thirsty as before you started.

1) Quantify Your Net Income

Above the entrance to the temple of Apollo in ancient Delphi were the Greek words *gnothi sauton* (γν□θι σεαυτόν), meaning "Know thyself." That's not bad advice, as oracular wisdom goes—but here is a more pragmatic directive:

Know thy income.

The first step in gaining control of your finances is to accurately identify how much net income you make—not gross, *net*.

For all practical purposes, your gross income is irrelevant because it is not fully available to you to spend. Net income—that is, income left over after deducting whatever expenditures it took to earn it *and* taxes—is what you can use to pay bills, save for the future, tithe to your church, invest, and so forth. Your net income is what you actually have to work with.

For example, let's say you have W-2 (wage) income from a job, 1099 income from a small home-based business, interest income from an investment, and babysitting income. Whatever it is, write it down, so you can determine your total monthly inflow. (Do this as a per-month figure; annual is too broad a picture to work with, and weekly is too narrow and variable.) Do not include "ifcome"—money from potential raises or bonuses or other *possible but not guaranteed* sources of income. If that bonus or new investment works out, great; that's gravy. For now, ignore it.

Next, deduct any business expenses and taxes. What is left over is your net income. (If you are an employee exclusively earning wage income, your net income is what your employer deposits every pay period.)

What you're really doing is applying resolution 6 to your finances: You are creating an accurate financial *scoreboard*. Without knowing exactly how much income you have to work with, you are running blind, which often leads to unwise choices. Don't guess or estimate. Get the facts down in black and white.

I have witnessed many radically positive changes take place in people's finances simply from their having the courage to start keeping score in their finances.

2) Quantify Your Expenses and Profit

The next step is to document your expenses—all of them. Write down anything that flows out of your possession into another entity's hands: all bill payments, all checks, cash, or charges. This includes whatever you spend on your car(s), house(s), clothing, meals, entertainment, kids' toys...*everything*. Again, add this up as a per-month figure.

Once you have accurately documented your monthly net income and monthly expenses, then *and only then* can you calculate your monthly profit:

Net Income – Expenses = Profit

And profit is key because profit, *not income*, is where your wealth is going to come from. This is so critical, and runs so strongly counter to what most people believe, that I need to repeat it once more:

Your wealth will not come from your income.
Your income is irrelevant.
Your wealth will come only from your profit.

The first time they do this, many people discover that they have no profit at all and may even be falling *behind* every month. Like a ship taking on water, this household is about to capsize.

If this describes your picture, then something has to change, and fast. You have to take action to get spending *below* net income. If spontaneous (read: frivolous) spending is an issue, then start setting aside a specific cash allowance for you and your spouse to spend on unplanned purchases, and don't exceed it...which brings us to a word you may not like, but need to hear: *budget*.

Many people viscerally resist the concept of a budget, but the truth is, you are already on a budget. The only question is whether you are willing to take an honest look at it and master it, rather than letting it master you. As with every one of life's scoreboards, putting your head in the sand does not change the lion's dinner plans.

The word *budget* comes from the Latin for *leather bag*. That's all a budget is: the finite bag of money you have to spend.

3) Set a Financial Goal

That topic of budgets brings us to the next step, which is to set a financial goal—not some pie-in-the-sky goal, not a goal for forty years from now, but an immediate, tangible financial target.

Here is a solid, doable financial goal you might start with:

Reduce expenses and increase income to the point where you are spending no more than 75 percent of your net income.

Don't worry if it takes time to achieve this goal. Start where you are. Honestly, the moment you get your spending below *100 percent* of net income is a cause for celebration.

When you spend every penny you make, you are like a bobber on the water's surface: the first big financial bite that comes along could pull your entire household under.

Setting and then reaching that 75 percent financial goal puts financial control in your hands. Every month you spend no more than 75 percent of net income, you are *saving* 25 percent of your net income, which is equivalent to one-third of your monthly expenses. This means that in just three months, you will accrue an amount equal to your monthly expenses and, therefore, *one full month* of genuine financial freedom. Over the course of one year, you will have "purchased" four full months of financial freedom.

This takes some tough thinking on your current financial position. Do you really need all the toys? Do you need the latest vehicle? Do you have to live in an expensive house?

The first time you seize control of your finances, the Joneses next door will assume you have suffered a severe setback and feel sorry for you. In truth, it's just the opposite. In finally confronting the facts and severing the chains of financial bondage, you are actually experiencing a surge ahead.

Don't bother trying to keep up with the Joneses. Whether or not they realize it, they are already broke.

4) Never Finance Anything That Depreciates

When asked what the greatest mathematical discovery of all time was, Albert Einstein replied, "Compound interest." Benjamin Franklin reputedly called compound interest "the eighth wonder of the world."

However, compound interest is a sword that cuts both ways, and it is razor sharp. It can cut through *anything*, especially your hard-earned money.

Paying interest on something that depreciates is a double whammy. You pay through the nose for borrowing money you don't have, and at the same time, you watch the asset you purchased lose its value. It's not uncommon for the asset to lose 50 percent of its value in a few years while you end up paying twice its retail value because of added interest payments.

Even if you have to purchase a major item on credit, seek to lower the borrowed amount and reduce the length of time for repayment as much as possible. The sooner you can pay off the mortgage on your property or loan on your car, the sooner you own the item. Up until that point, you're renting it from the bank.

Another deadly interest trap is the lease car option. When you lease a car, you don't actually *own* anything; you simply finance the car's depreciation and the car company's profits. And that's not even going into all the extra "gotchas" involved, such as the exorbitant fees the dealer levies if you go over your allotted mileage.

You have to decide which you love more: that new car or your financial freedom. Would you rather *look* successful— or *be* successful?

At the other end of the spectrum is buying a used car, especially for cash. This is a financial win in every way. First, the biggest reduction in a *new* car's price comes with its first few thousand miles, so you get to "buy low" after the new-car sheen—and hefty price tag—has worn off. You get much greater resale or trade-in value for your dollar. If you pay cash, you're not pouring out your hard-earned dollars in needless interest payments. And you're hanging onto thousands of dollars you can spend elsewhere, invest, or save.

5) Set a Price Limit on Spontaneous Purchases

We touched on this in the discussion of step 2 (quantify expenses), but it is so important that it deserves to be a step unto itself.

Spontaneous purchases are what kill most people's budgets. Billions of dollars are squandered every year by undiscerning buyers who make emotional decisions in the moment—and then pay for it for years. The solution?

*Set an absolute, agreed-upon price limit on all spon-
taneous purchases, and commit to the rule that the
decision to buy anything above this limit must be
slept on before purchasing.*

That twenty-four-hour "cooling-off" period is to help you
sort out whether that item is really worth the purchase, or
just something that will end up sitting in the garage. Often
by the next morning, the spell has broken, and you realize
that yesterday's urge to buy was a *want*, not a *must-have*.

Look at all the rummage sales where items are sold for
a tenth of their original price. Why reduce your wealth by
90 percent to buy things that will have no value in the long
run?

The specific amount of the price limit is a personal
family choice, but $100 is not unreasonable as a starting
point to help anchor this new behavior.

6) Shift from Credit to Cash

David Krueger describes an experiment conducted
by M.I.T. researchers in which consumers were allowed
to participate in a sealed-bid auction for Boston Celtics
basketball game tickets. Half were told that if they won,
they would have to pay in cash (with plenty of time given to
get the funds together). The other half were told they could
put the tickets on a credit card. Guess what happened?

The average of the bids of those who believed they
would be paying in cash was *half* the average bid
made by those who believed they would pay with a
credit card....When using a credit card, an expense
is only half as real as when paying cash.

Other studies have shown that spending increases by an average of more than 23 percent when
credit cards are used, as opposed to check or cash.

Credit card debt is one of the biggest sinkholes of American household finance. With their high interest rates and ease of use, they can quickly wipe out one's net worth. If you find you are spending more money when you use your credit cards, it's time to pay them off, cut them up, and shift to cash.

The only circumstances under which it makes any sense to use a credit card is when you can—and *do*—pay off the card balance in full every month. But if you are racking up debt, then having credit cards is a personal convenience in which you cannot afford to indulge.

7) Wipe Out All Consumer Debt

People often wonder whether, in the effort to get above water, they should start saving first or use that extra cash to pay down debt. Here is the answer:

Pay down debt first.

Imagine you are the captain of a ship, and you have just learned you're taking on water. Your response is clear: *All hands on deck!* You need every able-bodied effort to stop the leak and bail the water. You *must* stop the ship from sinking—that's priority one.

That ship is your household, and you need every dollar of disposable income to help bail out the debt before starting a savings plan.

Many people are saving money at 2 percent interest while carrying debt with an attached 20 percent interest. It doesn't take a Ph.D. in mathematics to figure out what that savings account is costing them: 18 percent!

Unless your savings account makes significantly more interest than your debt is costing, wipe out the debt first— and as fast as possible. Accelerate the house payments, sell off the toys, turn in the leased cars, and pay off the credit cards. Debt is cancer. The goal is to remove it as quickly as you can before it spreads and eats into healthy tissue.

The day you eliminate every last bit of debt is the first night you go to bed and wake up wealthier the next morning.

8) Understand the Difference Between an Expense and an Investment

It is good financial sense to cut all unnecessary expenses. On the other hand, you don't want to throw the baby out with the bathwater. A true expense simply consumes money—but an *investment* provides a *return* on that money.

Perhaps you've heard this joke:

Due to recent budget cuts and the rising cost of electricity, the light at the end of the tunnel has been turned off. We apologize for the inconvenience.

That's a pretty funny joke, but great companies understand the underlying principle very well. Even when cutting back on expenses, the best companies continue to do research and invest in the future. As individuals we must do the same.

Spending money to develop new skills is a good investment because those skills become part of who you are—no one can ever take that away from you—and they can enhance your capacity to earn future income. As Ben Franklin said:

An investment in knowledge always pays the best interest.

Never use lack of money as a reason not to invest in yourself. If you do, you are just telling your subconscious brain—your elephant—that the investment isn't worth it.

9) Focus on Quality of Life and Peace of Mind

Too many people, as they become wealthy, spend all their time attempting to increase their wealth, consigning their families, personal pursuits, and peace of mind to the backseat. Wise indeed are the words of Mark 8:36 (NKJV):

> For what will it profit a man if he gains the whole world, and loses his own soul?

As you grow wealthy, don't lose your focus. Pay attention to your quality of life and peace of mind, and don't squander attention on extraneous business interests or fall victim to others' grandiose schemes. Plans, like talk, are cheap; it's proper execution that makes businesses successful.

Here is a good rule of thumb: Never invest more money in someone else's business than you can comfortably afford to lose in its entirety. Otherwise, you will lose the quality of your life along with the money. Many people talk about diversification. Andrew Carnegie talks about *focus*:

> Put all your eggs in one basket, and protect the basket.

Remember resolution 1: follow your purpose into a field that cultivates your passions, potentials, and profitability.

10) Be a Blessing to Others

Following these nine steps, eventually you will reach the point where you are living today on money you made years ago. This is true financial freedom and peace of mind. And as this happens, you can invest more and more of your time and effort into being a blessing to others.

So many people suffer hardships along their paths. One of the most satisfying things a human being can do is to breathe confidence into another to help him overcome his obstacles. It has been said that man can live for forty days without food, four days without water, four minutes without air, but not four seconds without hope.

No matter how wealthy you become, you leave every dime behind when you die. Learning to pay your own financial blessings forward and serve the benefit of others by giving generously is a fundamental part of a successful, fulfilling life.

LEADERSHIP
"I resolve to practice the art and science of leadership."

The leaders who work most effectively, it seems to me, never say "I." And that's not because they have trained themselves not to say "I." They don't think "I." They think "we"; they think "team." They understand their job to be to make the team function. They accept responsibility and don't sidestep it, but "we" gets the credit.... This is what creates trust, what enables you to get the task done.
— Peter F. Drucker

The first four resolutions dealt primarily with private achievements, and the second set of four with public achievements. With resolution 9, we move beyond public achievement and into the realm of *leadership*.

Leadership is not a constant thing; it ebbs and flows in every organization depending on the character and competence of the individual leaders who are choreographing that organization's efforts.

Ask twenty people exactly what leadership is, and you may get twenty different answers. No matter how you define or describe it though, everyone knows when leadership is present—and when it's not.

One thing we know about genuine leadership: It is not about *me, me, me.* Leadership at the highest level demands a prevailing mindset of service to others, which requires a deep sense of empathy for others' strengths and weaknesses and a willingness to share the glory of triumph and recognition throughout the organization.

Michael Jordan is a great example of this kind of exceptional leadership.

In his basketball career, Jordan worked so hard and for so long that he reached the point where he had practically no limits—and then he took an eighteen-month sojourn in minor league baseball. By experiencing his own weaknesses in this new sport, he came to a deep understanding of the weaknesses of others for the first time in his career. Upon his return to basketball, his newfound empathy with his teammates moved him from being a good leader to a great leader.

As Aunt Elle, the mentor character in *It's Not About You*, puts it:

> The moment you begin thinking that it's all about you, that *you're the deal*, is the moment you begin losing your capacity to positively influence others' lives. In a word, to *lead*.

Business as a Game

In our discussion of resolution 5, we talked about the value of making your work into a game. Great leaders are skilled at doing this for the entire organization.

Business leaders treat their business as a game and all the participants as players on the team, knowing that people are naturally attracted to and engaged by the sense of healthy competition inherent in a good game. *The E-Myth* author Michael Gerber writes:

> People—your people—do not simply want to work for exciting people. They want to work for people who have created a clearly defined structure for acting in the world. A structure through which they

can test themselves and be tested. Such a structure is called a game. And there is nothing more exciting than a well-conceived game.

A business leader develops, defines, and sells the game to everyone in his community, and he must take care to define the game properly. Like any game, the business needs to have well-defined rules of engagement and rules for how to score points and win the game. Gerber elaborates:

> The degree to which your people "do what you want" is the degree to which they buy into your game. And the degree to which they buy into your game doesn't depend upon them but upon how well you communicate the game to them—at the outset of your relationship, not after it's begun.

To define the game, a leader decides which criteria are essential to satisfy the customers, and then turns these criteria into parameters of the game, so that playing the game successfully becomes synonymous with satisfying the customer base. This allows the team to keep score and reward those leaders and team players who execute the plays most effectively.

Another way of thinking about the game is to define the game plan through the litmus test we explored in resolution 1: *passion*, *potential*, and *profitability*. By clearly defining the three circles and updating them as conditions change to determine the intersection point of passion (*What are we passionate about?*), potential (*What can we be the best at?*), and profitability (*What drives our economic engine?*), you can ensure that your current game plan continues to be relevant and accurate.

Imagine two football teams that are both successful yet have different game plans based on how they see their core strengths (their version of passion, potential, and profitability). One team relies on a bruising ground game, while the other uses a lightning-quick passing game. Both win games following the same football rules, but each uses specific strategies based on its own Hedgehog Concept litmus test.

Playing a worthwhile business game brings meaning and purpose into people's lives, forming communities that play the game to win. Gerber explains:

> Part of what's missing is a game worth playing... What most people need, then, is a place of community that has purpose, order, and meaning.

Competition creates cooperation because winning the game becomes more important than each individual protecting his own perks and turf. This creates a sense of community, of team, as people focus together on achieving worthwhile results, producing meaning in their lives and satisfaction for the customers.

Like championship sports teams and elite military units, great business teams unify around common objectives, building relationships that last a lifetime.

Leaders Create a Cultural Current

In addition to defining the game, a leader must create a strong and cohesive *culture* in order to win the game. Organizational theorist Edgar Schein defines culture as:

> a pattern of shared basic assumptions that the group learned as it solved its problems that has worked well enough to be considered valid and is passed on to new members as the correct way to perceive, think, and feel in relation to those problems.

The culture determines how a group responds and solves problems in its quest to score points to win the game and satisfy its customers.

Culture is not a static thing, but a living, moving force. You can think of it as being like a powerful water current surging through a swimming pool. When new team members jump into the pool for the first time, they are pulled along in the direction the current is flowing.

What creates that current and determines the direction of its flow? One word: leadership. Typically, it is the beliefs and values of the entrepreneur who creates the business or organization that become the cultural principles of the institution. Ralph Waldo Emerson puts it this way:

> Every great institution is the lengthened shadow of a single man. His character determines the character of the organization.

When a leader jumps into the pool, he or she swims so powerfully that it generates a tidal current that influences everyone else in the pool—the rest of the team or community—to move in the same direction.

A strong sense of purpose, vision, and core principles will help align an organization's culture so that it not only runs in the desired direction but also carries new swimmers along until they learn to go with the current on their own. Without this cultural current in place, you'll have people going off in different directions, and suddenly the unity in the pool will start to disintegrate.

A vision-led culture drives a community's behavior better than a bureaucratic control-led culture ever will. Management expert Gary Hamel describes the difference:

> When it comes to mobilizing human capability, communities outperform bureaucracies...In a bureaucracy, the basis for exchange is contractual— you get paid for doing what is assigned to you. In a community, exchange is voluntary—you give your labor for the chance to make a difference, or exercise your talents. In a bureaucracy, you are a factor

of production. In a community, you are a partner in a cause. In a bureaucracy, "loyalty" is a product of economic dependency. In a community, dedication and commitment are based on one's affiliation with the group's aims and goals.

Leaders resist the temptation to try to control others, understanding that it is far more powerful to infuse community members with common goals and visions, and thereby align them toward the goal of achieving greatness together. Rather than seeking to control, they empower and unleash.

Changing Rules

There is, however, a key distinction between business teams and sports teams.

Leaders in sports win by developing and executing a game plan to consistently score more points than their competitors within the given structure of the game. The sports coach cannot change the rules; he can only develop and implement a better plan within those rules.

Business leadership is different. In a free-enterprise environment, the game is *not* predefined. Instead, it is developed by the organization's leaders by studying its customers' needs and competitors' strategies. What's more, at any time, a competitor can *change the rules of the game* and, in one stroke, make all former game plans obsolete. Because of this, an effective business leader must ensure that his strategy is always keeping abreast of the latest rules and game parameters.

Henry Ford changed the rules of the transportation game when he created his Model T automobile. No matter how good a manufacturer might have been at building horse carriages, Ford left him in the dust, forced to either play by the new rules or quit the game altogether.

Barnes & Noble changed the game of bookselling in the nineties by building a chain of gigantic stores where customers could not only browse for books but also sit with a cup of coffee and read. The sheer size of the new superstores also allowed them to carry massive inventory, creating a completely new set of customer expectations that most other stores could not hope to fulfill.

And then Jeff Bezos changed the game all over again with Amazon.com, offering books online with the ease of purchase from home—and an inventory even more massive than Barnes & Noble's.

Now Amazon is changing the game yet once more with its Kindle e-book device, and its competitors (including Barnes & Noble's Nook) are scrambling to catch up. With this latest shift in the game, a major transformation has come not only to book *shopping* but also to book *publishing*, and the traditional publishing houses are scrambling to avoid becoming obsolete. Whatever happens and however this plays out, one thing is for sure: the book business will never be the same again, thanks to an outsider who refused to play by the old rules.

Those businesses who strive to hold on to the glory of yesterday's game self-sabotage by holding fast to the "right way of doing things." Their customers, however, feel no such attachment and already have one foot out the door. They are heading over to shop with the competitors who have embraced a *new* right way of doings things.

With the dizzying rate of change today, as a business leader, you constantly need to scan the horizon, ensuring that the game you're currently playing is still satisfying your customers. In *Flash Foresight*, trend forecaster Dan Burrus writes:

> Reinventing oneself has always been a powerful strategy. But in the past, corporate and product re-invention was an *option*; today it is an *imperative*.
>
> In the old world, the rule was: "If it ain't broke, don't fix it."

In today's world, the rule is: "If it works, it's already obsolete."

A savvy business leader knows he needs to "break" his business before his competitors do.

The only constant in the game of business is the goal: satisfied customers. And the only way to achieve this goal is through continual and never-ending improvement, both in the game plan and in the game itself.

Trilateral Leadership Ledger and the Law of the Few

In our book *Launching a Leadership Revolution*, Chris Brady and I present a tool for becoming more effective leaders that we call the Trilateral Leadership Ledger (TLL).

Becoming a great leader requires growing in three areas: *character*, *tasks*, and *relationships*, or to put it another way, who you *are*, what you *do*, and how you *work with others*. The Trilateral Leadership Ledger measures each of these three quantities on a scale of 0 to 10 and then multiplies the three scores together to obtain a total score.

For example, let's say you rate yourself as a 4 in character, a 2 in tasks, and a 5 in relationships; your total score is 40:

$$4 \times 5 \times 2 = 40$$

Suppose you score yourself just as above, except with a 0 in relationships? Look what happens:

$$4 \times 5 \times 0 = 0$$

Scoring yourself with a 0 in *any one* of the three areas will bring your total score to 0, no matter how high you rate yourself in the other two areas, because anything multiplied by zero is going to be zero.

I've heard people say, "Well, I'm good at getting things done, and I have a solid character. But I'm just not a people person; I work better on my own."

Sorry, but that doesn't fly. As a leader, you cannot afford to say, "That just isn't me." You cannot ignore one facet in service of focusing on the other two. Leadership demands at least a passing grade in all three.

The TLL has helped tens of thousands of people grow in their leadership by identifying those areas where they most need improvement. The highest score mathematically possible is 1,000 (10 × 10 × 10 = 1,000). Since no human being is perfect, no one will ever achieve a score of 1,000. However, I have seen people score as high as 500. (For more on the Trilateral Leadership Ledger, refer to chapter 4 of our book *Launching a Leadership Revolution*.)

Becoming the One in a Thousand

Experience shows that only a minority—say, one in ten, or 10 percent—will excel in any one of these three attributes. A top leader, though, must excel in *all three*. Simple math tells the story of leadership: 10 percent × 10 percent × 10 percent = 1/10 percent, or 1 in 1,000.

In other words, on average, just one person out of a thousand exercises true leadership.

No matter what the community, organization, or business, a thousand people don't just spontaneously gather or come together out of some mysterious consensus. Instead, there is an individual, one out of the thousand, who causes them to gather together—one person who attracts, draws, and serves the other 999, without whom they would all go their separate ways.

That one person is a *leader*. As John Maxwell says:

Everything rises and falls on leadership.

Here is an odd bit of human nature: From my observations over the years of studying leadership, nine out of ten aspiring leaders are convinced that they are *already* among the top 10 percent of leaders. That is, 90 percent believe that they are in a place where, in fact, only 10 percent are.

If you say you're a leader, but when you turn around and look behind you, there's nobody following you, then I hate to break it to you, but you're just out for a walk.

The single biggest reason most leaders do not continue in their growth journey is that they believe they have already arrived. Good truly is the enemy of great.

UNITY
"I resolve to practice the art and science of conflict resolution."

To err is human, to forgive divine.
— Alexander Pope

As you build a following, whether you are leading a business, a church, or a charitable organization, you'll increasingly find yourself in situations where you will be called upon to resolve conflicts. In fact, conflict resolution is one of the most important arts of leadership, and one of the least understood.

The key thing to remember about conflicts is this: *They happen.* They are an inevitable part of human interaction. Just as every household generates garbage, every community and organization generates conflict. Every city has a plan for collecting, processing, and removing its garbage. In the same way, leaders must develop a plan for handling the conflicts that will inevitably arise.

Sitting on your garbage and simply allowing it to accumulate is no solution; neither is tossing a stick of dynamite at it. There needs to be a systematic, constructive process for dealing with the conflict so that it doesn't become toxic and start poisoning the whole community.

Conflict is like fire—relatively easy to snuff out when it's small, but nearly impossible to handle when it is allowed to spread unchecked. Imagine you're about to go to bed one night, and you happen to notice the flicker of a small flame in the corner of your room. What do you do? Tuck in and murmur, "Hope it's gone tomorrow," as you drift off? Of course not! You stop and put it out. Otherwise, you could wake up tomorrow without a home—or not wake up at all.

Silence or Violence

When conflict arises, one can *respond* by dealing with it constructively, or one can *react*, which generally means adding more fuel to the fire. There are two common ways that people react to conflict: with *silence* or with *violence*.

1) Silent Avoidance

Often people choose to avoid the issue rather than confront it head on. Instead of addressing the individual concerned, they silently nurse the hurt, building bitterness and resentment.

It has been said that holding onto bitterness and resentment toward another is like drinking poison and expecting someone else to die.

Sometimes we convince ourselves that if we don't confront it, the issue will simply go away. But here is a rule of thumb: if you think about a hurt more than once, it's time to address the issue.

2) Silent Denial

A variation of silent avoidance is to fool ourselves into thinking that the issue really isn't an issue at all, or that it is completely the other party's fault and therefore none of our concern. The frequency with which this happens is a testament to human beings' near-limitless capacity to deceive ourselves.

110

Denial of our own culpability allows us to place all the blame and responsibility for apologies and restoration on the other party—leaving ourselves only with the hurt. It also renders us powerless to do anything to ameliorate the situation. It's hard to fix something we claim isn't really there.

3) Silent Justification

The third common reaction people have to conflict is to argue it out silently, come to the conclusion that they were wholly in the right, and then use that conclusion as an excuse to dig in their heels, refuse to reapproach the relationship, and maybe even break off the relationship permanently.

Sometimes people even use silent justification as an excuse to quit the community or organization altogether.

This may be at least partially unconscious. It can feel like the path of least resistance; silent justification is easier than facing the issue out loud and in person. What's more, actively seeking resolution may require that we take a look at our own role in the events at issue, something people are often reluctant to do.

4) Violence

The choice to react to conflict with violence (and yes, it is always a *choice*) typically plays out in one of two ways. People either overtly attack others—confronting, accusing, shouting, and even physically hitting or worse—or they practice the more passive-aggressive (read: cowardly) approach of character assassination, attacking the person's reputation behind his back.

These two are not as different as one might think. Character assassination is just one level removed from actual, physical assassination.

More communities have been ruined by gossip than by any other behavioral issue. Gossip separates friends,

111

breaks trust, and makes resolution difficult. A popular story portrays the disastrous effects of gossip:

> A man with a troubled conscience went to a monk for advice. He said he had circulated a vile story about a friend, only to learn later that the story was not true.
>
> "If you want to make peace with your conscience," said the monk, "you must fill a bag with chicken down, go to every dooryard in the village, and drop in each one of them one fluffy feather."
>
> The man did as he was told and then returned and announced that he had done penance for his folly.
>
> "Not yet," replied the monk. "Now you must take your empty bag and gather up every feather you dropped."
>
> "But," the man stammered, "that's impossible! The wind will have blown them all away by now!"
>
> "True," nodded the monk. "And so it is with words. They are easily scattered—but no matter how hard you try, you can never gather them back again."

If someone starts running down another person in your presence, ask, "Can I quote you on this?" Stephen Covey explains:

> One of the most important ways to manifest integrity is to be loyal to those who are not present. In doing so, we build the trust of those who are present. When you defend those who are absent, you retain the trust of those present.

Don't Let Yourself Become Triangulated

When seeking to deal with a conflict, don't let yourself become a sounding board for any of the parties involved to simply vent—because if you do, you are just being drawn in and becoming a part of the conflict itself.

Congregational consultants Kibbie Ruth and Karen McClintock describe in their book *Healthy Disclosure: Solving Communication Quandaries in Congregations*:

> While people often suggest that venting is good for the soul, it is actually not very productive. Venting to someone about a third person is simply an avoidance technique that creates what is known in counseling theory as a relationship triangle, or *triangulation*.
>
> Triangulation is talking about feelings, opinions, or personal issues regarding some person or group with a third party instead of with the person or group actually concerned.

As Ruth and McClintock describe, the solution is to keep the focus on resolving the conflict, not on taking sides and furthering the scuttlebutt:

> The only way to stop the triangulation is for each person to communicate his or her feelings, concerns, or opinions directly to the other.

It's best to avoid being recruited into a triangle in the first place. Sometimes, though, no matter how well-intentioned we are, when listening to a person's concerns, feelings, or opinions, we suddenly realize we have inadvertently let ourselves be drawn into a situation and gotten involved, perhaps even to the point of taking sides.

Once you are in a triangle, it can take courage and clarity to escape, but it's doable. Redirect the concerned person straight to the appropriate individual or committee—the one who is actually involved in the issues or who can address the concern and/or mend the relationship.

A three-way conversation sometimes helps, but only if the third party facilitates without taking sides or having an agenda, without speaking for any of the parties, and without adding to the emotional drama.

Five Steps for Conflict Resolution

To resolve any conflict, both parties must be willing to sit down in person, face-to-face, to discuss the issue. This is crucial because we cannot pick up on the unspoken queues of body language over the phone or through email.

If either party does *not* agree to do this, then it is likely a signal that this person no longer values the relationship, or at least not enough to expend the time and effort to resolve the conflict. If that's the case, then there's probably not much you can do because no amount of effort from just one party will resolve the issue. It takes two or more to get into a conflict, and it takes these same parties to resolve it.

Once you have reached an agreement to sit down for an in-person meeting, here are the five steps:

1. Affirm the relationship.
2. Seek first to understand.
3. Then seek to be understood.
4. Own responsibility by apologizing.
5. Seek agreement.

1) Affirm the relationship.

The temptation is to start in right away on the issues. Don't do it! Before diving into the details of the conflict, it is essential that you first affirm the relationship.

The conflict is not why you're there to talk—the *relationship* is why you're there. In other words, the relationship is bigger than the conflict. Here is an example of an opening statement that conveys this:

I came here today, even though it's uncomfortable, because I value our relationship, and I would rather be uncomfortable resolving our misunderstandings than try to be comfortable living with the misunderstandings.

Let the other party know how important the relationship is to you.

The goal of this affirmation is for both parties to validate each other as human beings in a valued relationship. When hurtful issues are addressed later on, both sides should understand that the goal isn't to attack anyone but to address behaviors and underlying issues. People are affirmed, issues are addressed, and behavior adjustments are made to restore the relationship.

In *Crucial Conversations*, authors Joseph Grenny, Ron McMillan, Kerry Patterson, and Al Switzler address the importance of creating a safe environment where true communication flourishes by pouring all thoughts into a shared pool of meaning:

> When two or more of us enter crucial conversations, by definition we don't share the same pool. Our opinions differ. I believe one thing, you another. I have one history, you another.
>
> People who are skilled at dialogue do their best to make it safe for everyone to add their meaning to the shared pool even if the ideas, at first glance, appear controversial, wrong, or at odds with their own beliefs.

2) Seek first to understand...

After affirming the relationship, it's time to approach the conflict—and how you do this is critical. Even with that strong start, if you now begin explaining and justifying your own position, you lose ground—and you slip from *responding* to *reacting*.

The key is empathy. The objective is to listen intently, seeking to see the conflict from the other person's perspective, without any commentary or counterpoint on your part. Let the other person know you are there to listen and understand his thoughts and views. By providing the freedom for him to share his feelings and perspectives, you gain greater insight into how the conflict started, which helps in thinking through solutions to ensure better conduct in the future.

As you allow the other party to unburden himself, don't take his words personally. Don't react! Remember that people who are hurting can easily hurt others, even without meaning to. Hopefully, this step will help purge the other person of any bitterness building within him, at least to some degree.

After listening, repeat the person's concerns back to him, affirming them by summarizing what you heard. Genuinely listening to another person is one of the most affirming things you can do, and it will help *both* of you resolve any misunderstandings.

It is only after listening to the other party, asking questions to clarify and understand, that you can consider moving to the next step.

3) ...Then seek to be understood.

Now you're ready to respectfully share your own perspective on the issues. This can be trickier than you might think.

It's easy to say, "Okay, now let me tell you how it felt to *me!*"—and launch into "your side of the story." But your goal here is not to counter what the other person just said, and it's typically not productive to frame things in terms of "sides."

This is not a debate. The objective is not to determine that one was right and the other was wrong. The objective here is *resolution*.

This requires that both parties be honest about the part that each played in the conflict. No matter who did or said what, it always takes two to dance.

When you bring up the issues, don't assign motives to the other. For example, let's say you are hurt that your friend never called you when you were expecting him to. If you say, "It hurt my feelings that you would neglect me like that," you just left the realm of humanity and assumed the role of God.

Did your friend *intentionally* not call? Was it his purpose to neglect you? You cannot know. In fact, it's usually hard enough to discern our own motives, let alone claim to know the thoughts and motives of others!

Share the tough issues without generalizing or being dogmatic ("you always" or "you never"). Focus on the actions and behaviors, rather than the person and his motives. Give the other party as much benefit of the doubt as possible.

In most cases, your having taken the first two steps will by this time have made the other person feel more inclined to listen to you, too, with more openness and perhaps even a willingness to accept some responsibility for the conflict.

4) Own responsibility by apologizing.

The fourth step is to own as much of the conflict as possible while still being truthful. The objective is for both parties to see where one's actions caused pain to the other, leading to an apologetic spirit and a restored relationship.

Why do so many people struggle with apologizing for their hurtful actions? Perhaps it is because they are reluctant to admit their imperfection. But a genuine apology creates more good will than a thousand justifications will ever do.

Since we all know already that we aren't perfect, admitting this to others doesn't have to be a monumental revelation. In fact, the higher a person climbs the leadership ladder, the more he has to apologize to others simply because, as a leader, he juggles many things at the same time, which can lead to some being accidentally dropped. By apologizing, you will often restore trust in the relationship, better enabling you to explain what happened from your perspective without having to defend yourself.

5) Seek agreement.

Both parties have been affirmed, both sides have been heard, apologies have been made where appropriate, and now you're ready for the final step in the process, which is to look for agreement on where you go from here and how you will work together in the future in order to avoid further conflict.

The goal here is to unite and strengthen your relationship. The issues, having been flushed out of the relationship, leave only stronger bonds of love, trust, and unity.

Unity in a community creates harmony and good results; conversely, lack of unity in a community creates disharmony and decline. Leaders understand that conflict is a given, while resolution is a choice.

When you practice these five steps, not only will you resolve whatever issues arise, but you will also find that in the process, your friendships grow even stronger. When people realize that you value the relationship more than you value being "right," it builds trust. In fact, conflict resolution often turns out to create the most valuable opportunities to gain insight into your own blind spots and helps you build an even stronger community.

Relationships can bring so much joy into our lives—and by the same token, a damaged relationship can bring so much heartache. Mastering the ability to resolve a conflict quickly will improve your relationships, enhance your leadership, and enrich your life.

HOLISM
"I resolve to practice big-picture thinking."

To see a world in a grain of sand
And a heaven in a wild flower,
Hold infinity in the palm of your hand,
And eternity in an hour.
— William Blake

A fisherman went to the river to enjoy a day of fishing. Just minutes after settling in and getting his gear set up, he saw a young boy out in the middle of the river flailing his arms and screaming for help. The fisherman quickly jumped into the water, swam out, and pulled the boy to safety.

After the boy thanked him and went on his way, the fisherman resumed his fishing. Fifteen minutes later, he spotted a young girl out in the river struggling frantically and yelling for help. Jumping in, he saved her as well. Goodness, he thought, what were the odds that *two* children would need help on the same day in the same river?

After another fifteen minutes had gone by and a third child needing to be rescued came into view, the fisherman decided there had to be more to this picture than met the eye.

"I'm trimming the leaves of this tree," he told himself, "but I think it's time I found its roots."

After retrieving the third child, the fisherman began walking upstream. A few minutes later, he came to a children's day camp where he spotted a big kid by the river's edge threatening a smaller boy. "Give me your lunch money," the bully growled, "or I'll throw you in like the others."

The fisherman promptly took the bully by the ear and walked him to the camp counselor's office—after which, he enjoyed a quiet, contented afternoon of fishing.

If the fisherman in this story (courtesy of Stephen Covey) hadn't taken the time to go looking for the bully, he likely would have spent the whole day pulling kids out of the river and never gotten a lick of fishing in. And doesn't that describe what so many of us find ourselves doing? How often do we "solve" the problems on our plate by pulling distressed kids out of the river without ever walking upstream to find the root cause of the problem?

There is a term for what the fisherman did: he practiced *systems thinking*.

Seeing Systems

From the complex physiological systems that make up our bodies, to the natural systems of the ecology around us, to the complex human systems of which we are all a part, from family and friendship to community, nation, and globe, systems are everywhere.

A system is a *collection of connected elements in motion that adds up to more than the sum of its parts*. The key characteristic of a system is that you cannot understand how the system itself operates by examining only its discrete pieces: you need to look at the *whole*.

Peter Senge, in his classic book *The Fifth Discipline*, defines systems thinking and explains why it is such an important faculty in today's world:

Systems thinking is a discipline for seeing wholes. It is a framework for seeing interrelationships rather than things, for seeing patterns of change rather than static "snapshots."…

Today, systems thinking is needed more than ever because we are becoming overwhelmed by complexity. Perhaps for the first time in history, humankind has the capacity to create far more information than anyone can absorb, to foster far greater interdependency than anyone can manage, and to accelerate change far faster than anyone's ability to keep pace.…

Systems thinking is the antidote to this sense of helplessness that many feel as we enter the "age of interdependence."

Watch a team of mountain-climbers scaling a thousand-foot cliff, and you will see the systemic interdependence of all the climbers through the matrix of ropes and pulleys attaching each to the others. They are not a loose assortment of individuals, each acting on his own. No, they are a single smoothly-coordinated entity, and every action by any one of them profoundly affects the actions of all the others. No one climber can make it to the top on his own, and none will get there if even one decides to sit out.

The role of the leader in this human system is to direct all the climbers together to move safely and successfully up the cliff, and back down again. This is a balancing act because people are not machines and cannot be driven in the manner of an assembly line. If one climber tires, the leader may need to call a temporary halt because for one to rest, they all must rest. But if he allows one or more to slack, expecting the other climbers to make up for the difference, he hurts the team's performance and morale. And if he allows any one member to move along too quickly, that person will only exhaust himself and put the others at risk.

Even without physical ropes and carabiners, in any human organizational system, the interconnections are just as binding. Each person in a community needs to embrace a systemic mindset since his actions will affect all the others.

Yet not only is this kind of big-picture thinking more critical today than ever, as Senge says, but it is also *rarer* than ever.

In the modern era, detailed inquiry into specialized fields has helped to advance technological knowledge and improved quality of life by dividing the workload into manageable tasks—but this also has a downside. The fractionalization of knowledge caused by specialization has taught many to be experts in one species of tree while remaining clueless about the forest in which they live.

This is beautifully illustrated by the story of six blind men encountering an elephant for the first time. None of them has any idea what an elephant is, so they each reach out to touch the beast. One touches a tail and declares it is like a rope; one touches a leg and compares it to a tree. A third touches an ear and pronounces it similar to a fan; a fourth touches a tusk and says, "No, no, it is like a pipe," and so on. And they eventually fall into a bitter argument.

They are all right, to some extent—and they are all wrong. Each has grasped a partial truth of the elephant, but none has the whole picture.

How many issues in life stem from people arguing from their specific experiences, insisting on their version of truth because they are not seeing the big picture?

A Place to Move the World

The best businesses design systemic solutions to their customer's needs. Building a great business requires the design and implementation of a system that can produce consistent results for the customer without the need for extraordinary efforts. Systems guru Michael Gerber writes in his book *The E-Myth*:

You will be forced to find a system that leverages ordinary people to the point where they can produce extraordinary results. To find innovative solutions to the people problems that have plagued business owners since the beginning of time. To build a business that works. You will be forced to do the work of business development, not as a replacement for people development but as its necessary correlate.

Thomas Watson, the founder of IBM, understood systems thinking and sought to create a business model that would produce results long after he retired.

I realized that for IBM to become a great company, it would have to act like a great company long before it ever became one.

From the very outset, IBM was fashioned after the template of my vision. And each and every day, we attempted to model the company after that template. At the end of each day, we asked ourselves how well we did, discovered the disparity between where we were and where we had committed ourselves to be, and, at the start of the following day, set out to make up for the difference.

Every day at IBM was a day devoted to business development, not doing business.

Business systems make extraordinary results an ordinary occurrence. The secret is to learn where the leverage points lie within the system. Senge explains:

The bottom line of systems thinking is leverage— seeing where actions and changes in structures can lead to significant, enduring improvements. Often leverage follows the principle of economy of means: where the best results come not from large-scale efforts but from small, well-focused actions.

By studying systems thinking, a leader can learn the leverage points where he can create huge changes through small, seemingly insignificant adjustments. As Senge describes:

> Tackling a difficult problem is often a matter of seeing where the high leverage lies, a change which—with minimum effort—would lead to lasting, significant improvement.

Legend has it that when he discovered the principle of leverage, the great Greek mathematician Archimedes exclaimed:

> Give me a lever long enough and a place on which to stand, and I will move the world.

When his employer, the king of Syracuse, challenged him to prove his bold claim, Archimedes set up a demonstration in the Syracuse harbor, rigging together an elaborate system of ropes and pulleys. Then, using only the ordinary mortal strength of his arms—to the astonishment of the assembled crowd—he was able to move a great vessel weighing many tons.

Creating change on a vast scale requires leadership and leverage. A person cannot lift ten thousand pounds by himself, but with the right system, the same "impossible" task becomes doable.

A Balance of Duplication and Creativity

The key to the kind of leveraging business system Gerber describes is the *duplication* a finely crafted system can create.

Duplication reduces learning curves, increases output, and assures quality and effectiveness of the product or service.

For people to duplicate, leaders must discover what works consistently and then orchestrate those best practices throughout the organization's culture. As Gerber explains:

> Orchestration is based on the absolutely quantifiable certainty that people will do only one thing predictably—be unpredictable. For your business to be predictable, your people must be. But if people aren't predictable, then what? The system must provide the predictability. To do what? To give your customer what he wants every single time. Why? Because unless your customer gets everything he wants every single time, he'll go someplace else to get it!

If an organization is not duplicating, this means the leaders are not orchestrating the best practices across their communities. The plan is simple: Develop the patterns and systems to satisfy the customer, teach the patterns and systems to the employees, and reap the harvest of satisfied customers through a duplicable business system. Gerber adds:

> The system becomes a tool your people use to increase their productivity to get the job done. It's your job to develop that tool and to teach your people how to use it. It's their job to use the tool you've developed and to recommend improvements based on their experience with it.

However, one can take the idea of duplication too far. If it devolves into a mentality that says, "Just do it this way and don't think about it," then the team loses the creativity it needs to improve continuously.

A great idea to improve the system can come from anyone, and many times, it comes from the person who is responsible for a certain step in the process since he spends the most time doing it.

Finding the right balance between duplication and individual creativity is essential for long-term systemic results. Leaders work *on* the system and the team works *in* the system, but everyone needs to be constantly on the lookout for ways to improve.

The Japanese became famous for their system of *kaizen*, meaning "continuous improvement," which recognized and rewarded good ideas from anyone in the company who could help to improve their systems. Ray Stata, former CEO of Analog Devices, says:

> In the traditional hierarchical organization, the top thinks and the local acts. In a learning organization, you have to merge thinking and acting in every individual.

What One Person Can Do

Chaos theory tells us that slight changes applied to a leverage point in a nonlinear system can have massive results. This scenario is called the "butterfly effect," from the idea that something so small as a butterfly flapping its wings can cause a shift in atmospheric conditions, triggering a cascading series of events that results in a hurricane weeks later on the other side of the world.

The same thing happens in the mysterious climatic shifts of human affairs. Small, seemingly insignificant events can create subtle effects that lead to profoundly altered results. History is filled with examples of small incidents having a massive impact on the course of civilizations. The Great Courses series, taught by historian J. Rufus Fears, dramatizes this point:

- January 10, 49 B.C.: Julius Caesar crosses the Rubicon River into Rome, igniting a civil war that leads to the birth of the world's greatest ancient civilization.

- October 12, 1492: The Spanish explorer Christopher Columbus, weary after months at sea, finally drops anchor at the island of San Salvador and takes Europe's first steps into the New World.

- September 11, 2001: On a calm Tuesday morning, a series of terrorist attacks on the United States of America ignites a global war on terrorism that continues to this day.

History is made and defined by landmark events such as these—moments that irrevocably changed the course of human civilization. While many of us are taught that anonymous social, political, and economic forces are the driving factors behind events of the past, [I believe it is] individuals, acting alone or together, who alter the course of history.

A leader who embraces big-picture, systemic thinking learns how to *become* that butterfly.

This idea was exemplified by the life of inventor and philosopher R. Buckminster Fuller, one of the great systems thinkers of the twentieth century. When Fuller was still a young man, he reached a point of despair. His only daughter had just died, and he and his wife were not only grief-stricken but also broke and without prospects. Standing alone on the shore of Lake Michigan, Fuller contemplated ending his life.

Instead, he resolved to dedicate all his energy to exploring what a single human life might achieve:

Something hit me very hard, thinking about what one little man could do. Think of the *Queen Mary—*

the whole ship goes by and then comes the rudder. And there's a tiny thing at the edge of the rudder called a *trim tab*. It's a miniature rudder. Just moving the little trim tab builds a low pressure that pulls the rudder around. Takes almost no effort at all.

So I said that the little individual can be a trim tab. Society thinks it's going right by you, that it's left you altogether. But if you're doing dynamic things mentally, the fact is that you can just put your foot out like that and the whole big ship of state is going to go.

So I said, call me Trim Tab.

The larger the ship, the progressively more difficult it becomes to turn the rudder—and the more important the trim tab becomes. Senge explains why the trim tab is so appropriate for leverage in a system:

What makes the trim tab such a marvelous metaphor for leverage is not just its effectiveness, but its nonobviousness....So, too, are the high-leverage changes in human systems nonobvious until we understand the forces at play in those systems.

Train yourself to see the interconnectedness of the world around you and to think in terms of systems. Learn to see the trim tabs and butterfly wings in your organization.

The bigger the issues at stake, the more impact a single leader can have, and the more urgently he or she is needed.

RESILIENCE
"I resolve to increase my capacity to overcome adversity."

Fall down seven times, get up eight.
— Japanese proverb

Everyone gets knocked down; winners are those who get back up again.

The capacity to face and overcome adversity—to get back to one's feet after being knocked to the ground—is one of the most important traits that distinguish people who succeed in creating rich and purposeful lives from those who do not. All genuinely successful people have this trait in abundance, and no one who does *not* possess this trait in abundance—or learn to develop it—will ever experience significant and long-term success.

To describe this quality of character, I'm going to borrow the term *adversity quotient*, or AQ, from Paul G. Stoltz, PhD. In his landmark book *Adversity Quotient: Turning Obstacles into Opportunities*, Stoltz writes:

> Your success in life is largely determined by your AQ:

1. AQ tells you how well you withstand adversity and your ability to surmount it.
2. AQ predicts who will overcome adversity and who will be crushed.
3. AQ predicts who will exceed expectations of their performance and potential and who will fall short.
4. AQ predicts who gives up and who prevails.

If you implement all the other resolutions but fail in this one, then it will all unravel when things get turbulent. It is during the gloomy times, those days when everything seems to be going wrong, that both victors and victims are born. Which one you become in those moments depends on the choice you make: to persevere, or to give in.

Great leaders have unyielding perseverance in their quest for meaningful success.

What exactly *is* this elusive quality? Stoltz discusses the traditional capacity of IQ, a measure of intelligence, and EQ, the emotional counterpart to IQ introduced in 1995 by psychologist Daniel Goleman in his bestselling book *Emotional Intelligence*, and offers AQ as a crucial third dimension of character.

To these, however, I would add one more and propose that AQ is a combination of mental and emotional capacities, leavened with the driving force of *will*. Here is the formula:

$$AQ = IQ \times EQ \times WQ$$

In other words, your capacity to face and overcome adversity is equal to your intelligence (IQ), multiplied by your emotional maturity (EQ or *emotional* quotient), multiplied by your *will* quotient—that is, your drive to fulfill your purpose. Thus, AQ combines the strengths of the mind, heart, and will.

Smart Isn't Everything

Many people feel they are not smart enough to succeed, but typically the most successful people are *not* those who score highest on an IQ test.

For example, Henry Ford, the automobile magnate, although scoring off the charts in AQ, was no more than average in IQ. In fact, in a lawsuit between Ford and the *Chicago Tribune*, he showed that IQ was not the most important factor in a person's success. In *The Magic of Thinking Big*, David J. Schwartz writes:

> The *Tribune* asked him scores of simple questions such as "Who was Benedict Arnold?" "When was the Revolutionary War fought?" and others, most of which Ford, who had little formal education, could not answer.
>
> Finally he became quite exasperated and said, "I don't know the answers to those questions, but I could find a man in five minutes who does."…
>
> [Ford] knew what every major executive knows: that the ability to know how to get information is more important than using the mind as a garage for facts.

The beauty of the AQ formula is that you can make up for whatever deficits you have in one area by developing greater strength in another. Thus, even a person of average intelligence can, by developing great emotional maturity and applying great will, conquer any area and become an outstanding success. The key is to magnify your strengths and protect your weaknesses.

In fact, people with an especially high IQ often tend to overestimate their abilities, which can lead them to believe they are experts in areas where they actually need help. In *My Life and Work*, Ford writes:

None of our men are "experts." We have most unfortunately found it necessary to get rid of a man as soon as he thinks himself an expert—because no one ever considers himself an expert if he really knows his job. A man who knows a job sees so much more to be done than he has done, that he is always pressing forward and never gives up an instant of thought to how good and how efficient he is....The moment one gets into the "expert" state of mind a great number of things become impossible.

Ford understood that pure intelligence is not the principal ingredient in enduring success.

EQ: The Exercise of Neural Maturity

One day in September 1848, a young railroad worker named Phineas Gage was at the epicenter of an unfortunate accident. An explosion drove an iron rod straight through his head, destroying much of his left frontal lobe.

Amazingly, Gage survived the grisly event—but it soon became evident that he was not entirely the same man as he had been before. His normally steady, reliable temperament seemed to have vanished, and he would now lose his temper easily and become upset at the slightest provocation, cursing like a sailor when under stress and creating tension and chaos among his confused crew.

Gage's brush with death and subsequent personality changes made an enormous contribution to our modern understanding of brain function and what has come to be called *emotional quotient*, or EQ.

The neural pathways that carry input from the senses into the brain pass through the spinal cord into the back portion of the brain first, then move through the limbic system (the seat of feelings and emotions), and finally reach the frontal cortex (where we process rational thought). Since all sensory inputs travel through the limbic (feeling) area before reaching the rational brain, it's easy to react emotionally (especially to high-stress inputs) without allowing time to rationally develop a proper response. This is one reason we tend to buy on impulse before applying reasoned thought.

A high or well-developed EQ means we have learned to exercise the choice to think through issues before reacting. Despite the fact that input from our senses hits the "feeling" part of the brain first, with patience and intention, we can train ourselves to bring into play the frontal, rational brain in order to arrive at more appropriate, whole-brain responses to events—which is exactly what Phineas Gage was no longer able to do.

Of course, there was a clear reason for Gage's low EQ: He literally lacked the frontal lobe where reasoning and emotions combine; therefore, it was physiologically impossible for him to *think through* his feelings. But most of us have no such excuse.

No one enjoys associating with low-EQ people. It's hard to be friends with someone who can fly off the handle at the slightest provocation and seems to be at the mercy of the emotions of the moment without the capacity to think things through. People with low EQ have not mastered their own emotions. They have difficulty enough just leading themselves, let alone having the capacity to lead others.

A closely equivalent term for EQ would be *maturity*.

You can actively develop your EQ. Before reacting to stress emotionally, take a deep breath and will yourself to stay calm and nonreactive until you have the chance to reflect rationally and respond to the situation, instead of simply reacting to it. This will take practice, but the results are well worth the investment.

A low EQ by definition also lowers our AQ, making it significantly more difficult to face, manage, and overcome adversity.

All great victories in life begin with a victory over self.

Will Quotient and Learned Purposefulness

In 1965, Dr. Martin E. P. Seligman made a discovery that changed the face of twentieth-century psychology.

Prior to this time, psychology had been dominated by the deterministic ideas of behaviorism, which essentially proposed that human beings acted much like machines, with the nature of the stimulus dictating the nature of the response. This philosophy drew from the famous experiments of Pavlov (dog hears bell, salivates), and later the work of B. F. Skinner, and concluded that man lives largely by learned behaviors, leaving little room for thinking, responsibility, and change—that is, for the exercise of independent *will*.

Seligman's work challenged this central idea, ironically, with the discovery of what the scientist termed *learned helplessness*: the conditioned belief that what one does cannot alter one's outcomes, that somehow life's cards are stacked against him.

Seligman tested three groups of dogs in an experimental setup reminiscent of Pavlov, but with one crucial variation.

The dogs of group A heard a bell tone and then received an unpleasant (though harmless) electric shock, but they could stop the shock by pressing a bar with their nose, which they quickly learned to do. The dogs in group B heard the bell tone and received the shock, but they had no ability to stop the electric shock. The dogs in group C (the control group) received no shocks at all but simply heard the bell tone.

On the second day of testing, all the dogs from the previous day were placed, one at a time and in random order, in a box with a low barrier set up down the middle separating the electrically wired portion of the box from a neutral, "safe" area.

One by one, each dog heard the same bell tone and received the same shock. All the dogs from groups A and C quickly jumped over the barrier to get away from the mild discomfort of the shock, but the dogs from group B did not even try to jump and instead, simply crouched down and whimpered, accepting the continuing shock as their inescapable fate.

Stoltz describes the theory that came out of this experiment:

> What Seligman and others discovered is that these dogs had learned to be helpless, a behavior that virtually destroyed their motivation to act. Scientists have discovered that cats, fish, dogs, rats, cockroaches, mice, and people all are capable of acquiring this trait. Learned helplessness is simply internalizing the belief that what you do does not matter, sapping one's sense of control.

When a person believes that he cannot change his situation, he won't even try, becoming hopeless because he believes he is helpless.

Hopelessness, in other words, is a learned condition, and it is learned through a self-reinforcing vicious cycle: The less of a difference you think you can make, the less you try. And the less you try, the less of a difference you make.

What happened next is where it gets *really* interesting.

In the course of studying learned helplessness further, Seligman made another breakthrough discovery: Some people seem to exhibit a natural resistance to this trait, a sort of hard-wired refusal to give in to hopelessness, regardless of stimuli or circumstance. He dubbed this trait *learned optimism*: the attitude that says, with the right knowledge and attitude, applied consistently and persistently, we can change nearly *anything*.

As exciting as this concept is, I would take it one step further because the state I am seeking to describe here is more than a good mood or positive outlook—it is what lies *behind* that positive outlook.

The inverse of learned helplessness is a trait I would call *learned purposefulness*.

Another term for this dimension of character would be *will*—that fundamental capacity that allows us to control our actions and align them with our intentions, irrespective of external factors. Having a strongly developed will is what enables us to consistently *do* what others only talk about doing.

Harland Sanders: Profile in AQ

Broke at the age of sixty-five, Harland Sanders, an Indiana native transplanted to Kentucky, had just sold his little restaurant and hit a financial dead end. He cashed his $105 Social Security check, used every penny of it to develop his chicken recipe, and then hit the road, going from restaurant to restaurant in the effort to sell his recipe. He was turned down, not by dozens, not just by hundreds, but by slightly more than *one thousand* restaurants before securing the franchises he needed to become viable. This took several years, during which he slept in the backseat of his car.

Imagine doing what Sanders did, in your sixties, with absolutely no external evidence that you would ever succeed. How many nos would you suffer through before calling it quits? Twenty? Fifty? Two hundred?

Sanders was able to persevere and eventually create a multimillion-dollar food empire for one and only one reason: his off-the-charts AQ. He applied the PDCA process to his efforts over and over until he got it right, eventually founding one of the most successful franchises in the world today.

In every worthwhile endeavor, there is an incubation period, a time when, even though you may be doing everything right, the results are simply not there yet to *prove* you right. "Faith is the substance of things hoped for," says the author of Hebrews, "the evidence of things not seen" (Hebrews 11:1 NKJV), and AQ is the working of that faith in action over time.

If you compromise at any point during that crucial incubation period, success will never reveal its secrets. AQ is what keeps you in the game long enough to start seeing the fruits of your labors. Without it, not only are the odds stacked against you, but the game itself is rigged for you to lose.

Looking backward with the eyes of hindsight, the ultimate success of Colonel Sanders's enterprise seems foreordained, an inevitability. We here in the twenty-first century know that Sanders's recipe, near-fanatic attention to quality, and franchise model would make KFC a household word. But in the early 1950s, when he was criss-crossing the country struggling to sell his franchise rights and earning back a nickel for each chicken sold, there was nothing inevitable about it.

Indeed, it looked downright impossible. But he had *the evidence of things not seen* going for him—that, and exceptional AQ.

LEGACY
"I resolve to leave a legacy by fulfilling my purpose."

What is the use of living, if it be not to strive for noble causes and to make this muddled world a better place for those who will live in it after we are gone? How else can we put ourselves in harmonious relation with the great verities and consolations of the infinite and the eternal?
— Sir Winston Churchill

The last resolution ties together all the others, and it has to do with something that ties together everything in your life.

The word *legacy* is most commonly used to refer to the money one leaves behind at death—but that is not the meaning at the core of the thirteenth and final resolution. Let's take a closer look at the heart of the word.

Legacy comes from the Latin word *lex*, meaning "law or contract," the same root word behind the terms *legal*, *delegate*, and *elect*. Your legacy is your legal representative, your delegate, the ambassador that you elect to leave behind and represent you in this world when it comes time for you to move on to the next. It is the substance of your impact on and contribution to the world; in a word, it is the *difference* your being here has made.

The Syntropic Force of Legacy

Have you ever noticed that there seems to be a natural tendency toward decline in just about everything around us? For example, look at your room—your bedroom, kitchen, living room, office, any room where you spend a lot of time. Unless you make a concerted effort to prevent it, doesn't the room naturally grow messier over time, rather than neater? Left on its own, a house spontaneously becomes dirtier and more disorderly, not cleaner and more orderly.

There is a reason for this, a natural law that scientists term *entropy*: the tendency of all systems to lose structure and energy and trend toward collapse. Things break down. Order decays. All living things age and then die, their marvelous complexities breaking down into the simplest elements.

This is also true in the world of human affairs. It requires little effort for things to deteriorate but rigorous discipline for them to consistently improve. Even the most successful organizations do not last forever, including the largest of human organizations, our very civilizations themselves. Civilizations as diverse as the Sumerians, Egyptians, Persians, Greeks, Romans, and Chinese all declined, eventually falling under their own weight.

Why do even the greatest civilizations seem to fall? Is this simply the natural condition of life, an ineluctable edict from which nothing can escape?

The answer turns out to be yes...and no. Yes, the law of entropy does inescapably govern every phenomenon in the universe. But does that mean all efforts to improve our lot and build something both great and lasting are doomed to fail?

The great British historian Arnold J. Toynbee didn't think so. In his multi-volume classic on the history of world civilizations *A Study of History*, Toynbee details the rise and decline of twenty-three civilizations. Despite detecting uniform patterns of disintegration in each civilization,

Toynbee insists that leaders have a capacity—and a moral responsibility—to counter and end the cycle of decline. As Jurgen Schmandt and C. H. Ward write in *Sustainable Development: The Challenge of Transition*:

> Toynbee reserved the terms "challenge and response" for major threats and actions that impacted the well-being of the entire population. "Challenge" threatened the very survival of the existing system. "Response" would range from inaction to major change in the living conditions of individuals as well as the group. It could embody new technology, social organization, and economic activities, or a combination of various factors. "Response" was never predictable, and its outcome would only be known over time. This was the risk humans took—resulting in success or failure.

According to Toynbee, the growth or decline of civilizations is based not on immutable and impersonal historical forces but on leadership capabilities present in society. Unlike the deterministic Oswald Spengler, who in his *The Decline of the West* treats civilizations as unalterable machines following predictable cycles of decline, Toynbee viewed them as networks of social relationships susceptible to leadership decisions.

Toynbee's historical analysis focused on the spiritual, economic, and political challenges in civilizations, and posited that it was the role of leaders—what he termed "creative minorities"—to respond to the challenges in order to sustain a civilization's progress. A civilization declines, in other words, when its leaders fail to respond creatively to the challenges faced. When this happens, according to Toynbee, the civilization sinks under nationalism, militarism, and the tyranny of a despotic minority:

> Civilizations die from suicide, not by murder.

It is the ultimate challenge of a leader to create a momentum that brings about a *decrease* in entropy.

Buckminster Fuller identified this balancing, constructive, synthesizing force and named it *syntropy*: entropy's mirror opposite, a creative tendency toward increasing order, complexity, and functionality. He went on to hypothesize that it is the purpose of humanity to act as a counterfoil to the natural currents of entropy—to be the universe's representative of the force of syntropy.

Fuller's insight provides us with a concise job description for leaders. A great leader is syntropy's representative on earth: one who overcomes the degenerative tendencies inherent in all human communities and organizations by creating a culture-current of progress that extends the life and vitality of his organization far into the future, even well beyond his own mortal life span—in some cases, for centuries.

That is the ultimate definition of legacy.

The Five Laws of Decline

In order to gain a fuller understanding (pun intended) of the power and significance of legacy, let's take a moment to explore just what it is we're up against.

As a systems engineer, I have made an extensive study of leadership teams, organizations, and cultures throughout history, and have found untold numbers of similar patterns of failure and decline at work. To help understand exactly how this happens, I have assembled a set of five laws of decline as a systems model that explains why civilizations, nations, and communities fail and fall. Each of these five laws provides a slightly different perspective on those entropic forces that systematically flow against all progress, much the way gravity works to ground all flying objects.

These five laws do not mean that we *can't* fly—but if we want to soar, we'd better first understand the nature of gravity!

1) Sturgeon's Law

At the 1953 World Science Fiction Convention, the great science fiction writer Theodore Sturgeon responded to the many critics of his beloved genre with this statement:

> I repeat Sturgeon's Revelation, which was wrung out of me after twenty years of wearying defense of science fiction against attacks of people who used the worst examples of the field for ammunition, and whose conclusion was that 90 percent of science fiction is crud. Using the same standards that categorize 90 percent of science fiction as trash, crud, or crap, it can be argued that 90 percent of film, literature, consumer goods, etc. are crap. In other words, the claim (or fact) that 90 percent of science fiction is crap is ultimately uninformative, because science fiction conforms to the same trends of quality as all other art forms.

Elsewhere Sturgeon put what he came to call Sturgeon's Law more concisely:

> Ninety percent of [science fiction] is crud—but then again, so is ninety percent of *anything*.

We saw this in our exploration of leadership in resolution 9: only one in ten will excel in any of the key attributes of leadership. This doesn't mean the other nine people are "crud," only that there is a natural tendency for the majority to slide to the lower end of any achievement scale—almost a gravitational pull toward mediocrity against which the drive for excellence must struggle in order to...well, to *excel*.

Leaders cannot beat Sturgeon's Law, but they can create a culture that attracts the 10 percent who choose to lead and thus develop a culture that rewards performance, not politics. Communities advance when their leadership positions are filled by the 10 percent who excel and decline when those leadership spots are assumed by people from the 90 percent—the "trash, crud, or crap," as Sturgeon so bluntly put it—who are incapable of reversing the entropic tendency toward decline and disintegration.

Alexander the Great understood this thousands of years ago when he declared:

> An army of sheep led by a lion is better than an army of lions led by a sheep.

2) Bastiat's Law

In his book *The Law*, French economist Frédéric Bastiat describes a fatal tendency in man's heart to satisfy his wants with the least possible effort, leading inevitably to the exploitation of others:

> Man can live and satisfy his wants only by ceaseless labor; by the ceaseless application of his faculties to natural resources. This process is the origin of property.
>
> But it is also true that a man may live and satisfy his wants by seizing and consuming the products of the labor of others. This process is the origin of plunder.
>
> Now since man is naturally inclined to avoid pain—and since labor is pain in itself—it follows that men will resort to plunder whenever plunder is easier than work. History shows this quite clearly. And under these conditions, neither religion nor morality can stop it.

Therefore, Bastiat concluded, much of history is a record of man's plundering of his fellow man, and the only way to counter this natural slide towards plunder is through the collective application of laws to protect property and punish plunder.

Bastiat's Law eloquently exposes the fatal flaw in the theory of communism, since the 90 percent will do as little as possible if given the opportunity, while the 10 percent are driven to despair since they aren't rewarded for their productive efforts.

The only proven way to combat Bastiat's Law is to develop, score, and reward performance in the game of business.

3) Gresham's Law

Gresham's Law, named for the British financier Sir Thomas Gresham, originally applied to monetary policy. American economist Murray Rothbard states it like this:

> When government compulsorily overvalues one money and undervalues another, the undervalued money will leave the country or disappear into hoards, while the overvalued money will flood into circulation.

For example, when inflated paper money flows into the marketplace, real gold and silver coins are removed from the marketplace. No one willingly pays for goods and services with real money when paper is made a legal currency by government fiat. Real money remains out of circulation until the paper fraud runs its course.

The same principle applies to other fields: Bad education drives out good education, bad leadership drives out good leadership, and poor character drives out good character, to name just a few. It occurs in companies when political managers are promoted ahead of productive leaders.

Gresham's Law is often summed up by the catchphrase "bad money drives out good" and, in its broader application, might be succinctly stated this way:

Lower quality drives higher quality out of the marketplace.

What is rewarded will increase; conversely, what is *not* rewarded will decrease. When the poor behaviors are rewarded, the company is quickly filled with others exhibiting the same nonproductive activities—and productive leaders, unwilling to play the political games of a declining culture, are driven out of the company.

Getting the right people *on the bus* and *in the right seats*, to use Jim Collins's terms, is the only way to ensure that the 90 percent do not infiltrate and eventually take over the company.

4) Law of Diminishing Returns

One of the most fundamental laws of modern economics, the Law of Diminishing Returns states that:

After a certain level of performance has been reached, continuing in that activity will result in a decline in effectiveness.

In other words, once you reach a certain point of production, your returns begin to decrease, and they continue decreasing as production continues, assuming all other variables are held constant.

For example, by adding a pound of fertilizer to a garden, tomato production goes up. Adding another pound of fertilizer increases production even further. But at some point, adding more stops increasing production and even starts to *decrease* production, as too much fertilizer burns the plants.

The Law of Diminishing Returns affects the quality of anything when one attempts to produce its benefits on a large scale. You can see the results of this law, for example, in tourism, as author Wendy McElroy describes in her essay "Nock on Education":

> Consider the everyday experience of vacationing at a location that has not yet been "discovered" by floods of tourists. When tourists begin to flock to the location, the return to everyone abruptly decreases....In accommodating popular demands, the vacation site (and all other experiences in life) fall prey to the law of diminishing returns.

Albert Jay Nock describes the same phenomenon in the field of education:

> Socrates chatting with a single protagonist meant one thing, and well did he know it. Socrates lecturing to a class of fifty would mean something woefully different, so he organized no classes and did no lecturing.
> Jerusalem was a university town, and in a university every day is field-day for the law of diminishing returns. Jesus stayed away from Jerusalem and talked with fishermen here and there, who seem to have pretty well got what He was driving at; some better than others, apparently, but on the whole pretty well.

In other words, an increase in *quantity* invariably leads to a decrease in *quality*.

5) Law of Inertia

Isaac Newton's famous first law of motion states:

> Every body remains in a state of rest or uniform motion (constant velocity), unless it is acted upon by an external force.

In layman's terms, an object at rest tends to stay at rest, and an object in motion tends to stay in motion unless acted upon by another force—in a word: *inertia*.

Inertia works in the pool when the current carries people in the direction of the flowing water. When a leader is confronted with the task of reversing the direction of the current in the pool, he has to work not only to move in the new direction but also to overcome the inertia of the current that is still moving in the other direction.

What's more, the longer the current has been allowed to flow in one direction, the more difficult it is to reverse that direction because of the greater buildup of inertia that must be overcome.

It's hard enough to create a strong new current in a pool of still water, but establishing that strong new current in a pool where you first have to reverse an old, unproductive current is an enormously more difficult challenge. Yet this is exactly what most leadership assignments demand.

This is why turnaround experts in business are so highly valued and why successful turnarounds in big companies are so rare. Leaders who take over declining businesses have to struggle against the distracting habits, dysfunctional processes, and destructive attitudes in their efforts to turn around the unhealthy culture and create a healthy one.

A Legacy of Leadership

These five laws of decline make it easy to understand why there is such a strong gravitational drag working against all organizational progress and, thus, why organizations eventually fall. In due time, Sturgeon's Law will eventually place 90-percenters in the top positions rather than 10-percenters, and these weak leaders will allow the wrong people on the bus, driven by their inclination to plunder the efforts of others, as Bastiat's Law describes. Following Gresham's Law, the proliferation of these weaker players will in time drive out the stronger leaders, and just as a snowball rolling downhill gathers momentum, the twin forces of inertia and the Law of Diminishing Returns will aggravate the decline.

If a 10-percent leader—or as is increasingly necessary, a 1-percent or 0.1-percent (the one in a thousand) leader—does not appear soon and start reversing the culture before it's too late, the current of entropy will pick up speed and momentum, becoming unstoppable, and ultimately, the organization will dissolve into nothing.

You've seen it happen to great companies, great families, and great cities. It can even happen to great countries.

However, there is a solution. Leaders can overcome these forces of decline by implementing the thirteen resolutions in their lives and organizations. The biggest gift one generation can give to the next is a legacy of leadership.

As you learn financial principles that make a difference in your life (resolution 4), document and share them with as many people as possible. Likewise, as you learn friendship principles that help you build strong, long-term relationships (resolution 7), or tools for resolving conflicts that arise within your community (resolution 10), then share those principles with others. Any area where you learn and apply sound principles and produce good fruit in your life is a platform for leaving a legacy for others.

The difference between leaders and followers is that leaders take responsibility for the direction of the current in the pool. Leaders follow an inner compass to determine which direction the current should be flowing and then take a stand against the prevailing current and, when necessary—as it so often is—against the crowd that is flowing with it.

Standing against such a current is an act of courage—and one that by definition is committed by only the rare minority. As the saying goes:

Any dead fish can float downstream, but it takes a live one to swim against the current.

And yet it does not take more than those few to counteract the impact of the five laws of decline and reverse the destructive, entropic current in the pool of humanity. Doing so is the greatest gift any of us can leave for future generations—a legacy truly worth leaving for posterity.

POSTSCRIPT

A Personal Note

The subject of this book is near and dear to my heart; indeed, it is what I have devoted my life to, for I believe in my heart of hearts that the world deeply and desperately needs individuals like you to *take* these principles to heart and enact them in exemplary lives of legacy.

Leadership is not for the weak of heart (to use the word "heart" yet one more time!) because every leader must make decisions that are not likely to endear him to all parties involved. Yet decide he must, if he plans on leading. Being a leader in today's often selfish and cynical world can cause anyone living the thirteen resolutions to be portrayed as being out of touch or irrelevant. This is tragic irony: the world so often denies the principles of character, honor, and purpose—yet it is quite literally dying for lack of them.

Without "challenge and response" leadership, as we spoke about in our exploration of resolution 13, all civilizations fall into decline. In fact, in his classic text *The Decline and Fall of the Roman Empire*, Edward Gibbon defines five attributes that marked the Roman Empire at the time of its fall over 1,500 years ago:

1. A mounting love of show and luxury (affluence);
2. A widening gap between the very rich and the very poor;
3. An obsession with sex;
4. Freakishness in the arts, masquerading as originality;
5. An increased desire to live off the state.

Even a perfunctory examination of contemporary society reveals a worrisome prevalence of all five attributes.

In his 1920 poem, "The Second Coming," W. B. Yeats conveyed the sense of hopelessness that prevailed in Europe in the aftermath of the First World War, a hopelessness that in my observation is all the more prevalent today:

> Things fall apart; the centre cannot hold;
> Mere anarchy is loosed upon the world,
> The blood-dimmed tide is loosed, and everywhere
> The ceremony of innocence is drowned;
> The best lack all conviction, while the worst
> Are full of passionate intensity.

Gibbons's observations and Yeats's words both describe the impact that the five laws of decline unleash upon a leaderless world.

Yet this current of decline can still be reversed.

For the last eighteen years, I have communicated this message to millions of people across North America through a leadership and personal development training community now called the LIFE business. The members of this community are dedicated to forging the thirteen resolutions in our being and, thus, reversing the currents of decline both for our time and for future generations. This community has witnessed the lives of numerous downtrodden and depressed people turned around through the power of faith, hope, love, and leadership.

To borrow Toynbee's words, the *Challenge* is clear, and this is our *Response*:

> We have resolved to respond to the distress call, dedicating our lives to reversing the current of decline.
>
> Will you help us?

LIFE
SUBSCRIPTIONS

LIFE SERIES

Our lives are lived out in the eight categories of Faith, Family, Finances, Fitness, Following, Freedom, Friendship, and Fun. The monthly LIFE Series of 2 CDs, 1 DVD, and a book is specifically designed to bring you life-transforming information in each of these categories. Whether you are interested in one or two of these areas, or all eight, you will be delighted with timeless truths and effective strategies for living a life of excellence, brought to you in an entertaining, intelligent, well-informed, and insightful manner. It has been said that it may be your life, but it's not yours to waste. Subscribe to the LIFE Series today and learn how to make yours count!

The LIFE Series – dedicated to helping people grow in each of the 8 F categories - Faith, Family, Finances, Fitness, Following, Freedom, Friendship, and Fun.
2 CDs, 1 DVD, and a book shipped each month.
$50.00 plus S&H
Pricing valid for both USD and CAD

LLR SERIES

Everyone will be called upon to lead at some point in his or her life, and often, at many points. The issue is whether or not people will be ready when called. The LLR Series is based upon the *New York Times* bestseller *Launching a Leadership Revolution*, written by Chris Brady and Orrin Woodward, in which leadership is taught in a way that applies to everyone. Whether you are seeking corporate or business advancement, community influence, church impact, or better stewardship and effectiveness in your home, the principles and specifics taught in the LLR Series will equip you with what you need.

The subscriber will receive 2 CDs, 1 DVD, and a leadership book each month. Topics covered will include finances, leadership, public speaking, attitude, goal setting, mentoring, game planning, accountability and tracking of progress, levels of motivation, levels of influence, and leaving a personal legacy.

Subscribe to the LLR Series and begin applying these life-transforming truths to your life today!

The LLR (Launching a Leadership Revolution) Series – dedicated to helping people grow in their leadership ability.
2 CDs, 1 DVD, and a book shipped each month.
$50.00 plus S&H
Pricing valid for both USD and CAD

Don't Miss Out on the 3 for FREE Program!

As a Customer or Member subscribes to any one or more of the packages, that person is given the further incentive to attract other Customers who subscribe as well. Once that Customer or Member signs up three or more Customers on equivalent or greater dollar value subscriptions, the Customer or Member will get his or her next month's subscription FREE!

AGO SERIES

Whether you have walked with Christ your entire life or have just begun the journey, we welcome you to experience the love, joy, understanding and purpose that only Christ can offer. This series is designed to touch and nourish the hearts of all faith levels as our top speakers, along with special guest speakers, help you enhance your understanding of God's plan for your life, your marriage, your children, and your character, while providing valuable support and guidance needed by all Christians. Nurture your soul, strengthen your faith, and find answers on the go or quietly at home with the AGO Series.

The AGO (All Grace Outreach) Series – dedicated to helping people grow spiritually.
1 CD and a book shipped each month.
$25.00 plus S&H
Pricing valid for both USD and CAD

EDGE SERIES

Designed especially for those on the younger side of life, this is a hard-core, no frills approach to learning the things that will make for a successful life.

Eliminate the noise around you about who you are and who you should become. Instead, figure it out for yourself in a mighty way with life-changing information from people who would do just about anything to have learned these truths much, much sooner in life! It may have taken them a lifetime to discover these truths, but what they learned can be yours now on a monthly basis.

Edge Series – dedicated to helping young people grow.
1 CD shipped each month.
$10.00 plus S&H
Pricing valid for both USD and CAD